ECONOMIC AND SOCIAL COMMISSION FOR ASIA AND THE PACIFIC

IMPROVING THE ACCESS
OF WOMEN TO FORMAL CREDIT
AND FINANCIAL INSTITUTIONS:

WINDOWS OF OPPORTUNITY

VOLUME II

UNITED NATIONS
New York, 1997

ST/ESCAP/1859

UNITED NATIONS PUBLICATION
Sales No. E.98.II.F.40
Copyright © United Nations 1997
ISBN: 92-1-119829-1

PREFACE

This publication is an outcome of the project entitled "Improving the access of women to formal credit and financial institutions in selected least developed countries of the Asian and Pacific region". The objectives of the project were: (a) to evaluate the potential of, and constraints faced by, women in obtaining credit from formal financial institutions; (b) to identify special features of successful formal credit programmes; and (c) to formulate recommendations to improve access by women to formal credit and financial institutions.

During the first phase of the project, national studies on five least developed countries (Bangladesh, Bhutan, the Lao People's Democratic Republic, Myanmar and Nepal), four developing countries (India, Indonesia, Pakistan and Thailand) and a regional overview study were prepared. From the overview and country studies, the publication entitled *Improving the Access of Women to Formal Credit and Financial Institutions: Windows of Opportunity* was issued in 1995. At the end of the first phase of the project, an expert group meeting was convened in Bangkok from 14-16 November 1994. A recommendation made at that meeting was for a series of national workshops to be organized in selected least developed countries, followed by a regional seminar.

A national workshop held in Thimpu, Bhutan, from 11-14 December 1995 in cooperation with the Bhutan Development Finance Corporation, centred on strengthening rural credit and finance as the difficulties encountered in obtaining rural credit and their solutions were similar to those related to access by women to formal credit and financial institutions. The Agricultural Development Bank of Nepal acted as the counterpart for a national workshop held in Kathmandu from 9-12 July 1996. At that workshop it was noted that a lack of formal ownership of assets as a major impediment to access by women to credit. The Governor of the Bank of the Lao People's Democratic Republic acted as chairperson in a national workshop which was held in Vientiane from 23-24 August 1996. The workshop followed the Roundtable on Microfinance, held on 22 August 1996, which was organized jointly by the Ministry of Finance of the Lao People's Democratic Republic, the United Nations Development Programme and the United Nations Capital Development Fund.

A regional seminar was held in cooperation with the Vietnam Bank for Agriculture and Rural Development (VBARD) in Hanoi, from 1 to 4 July 1997, to enable selected institutions providing both formal and semi-formal credit to women in least developed countries to exchange views and to consult experts in the field. Representatives from central banks, rural development banks, non-governmental organizations and national women's associations in Bangladesh, Bhutan, Cambodia, the Lao People's Democratic Republic, Maldives, Myanmar, Nepal and Viet Nam attended the meeting. Among the issues discussed at the regional seminar were current policies, procedures and practices in lending by formal credit and financial institutions, legal issues such as collateral issues, and the relationship between donor agencies and the financial institutions.

This publication has three parts. Part One lists the recommendations made at the regional seminar. Part Two discusses recent developments in policies and practices aimed at improving access by women to formal financial institutions. It also summarizes country experiences as presented at the regional seminar. Part Three, prepared by VBARD, is the country study on Viet Nam. It focuses on the modalities used by formal financial institutions, notably VBARD and the Vietnam Bank for the Poor (VBP) to deliver credit to women living primarily in rural areas.

The recommendations made at the regional seminar for improving access by women to formal credit and financial institutions, as noted below, were formulated by participants who represented a wide range of institutions in least developed countries of Asia. The recommendations were developed through: (a) the review of the various experiences in the least developed countries as well as other developing countries; (b) discussions during the various sessions of the regional seminar; and (c) consultations with experts. Some of the recommendations were also refined by drawing on the conclusions drawn in the national workshops. The recommendations should therefore be applicable to a wide range of countries at different stages of economic and social development in the region. It is hoped that member countries will take the recommendations into consideration when formulating appropriate policies for improving access by women to formal credit and financial institutions.

The ESCAP secretariat would also like to take this opportunity to express appreciation to the Government of the Netherlands for its continued support for the project.

CONTENTS

LIST OF TABLES

LIST OF FIGURES

LIST OF BOXES

READERSHIP SURVEY

1. It was noted that an enabling environment is necessary in order to improve access by women to formal credit and financial institutions. Such an enabling environment requires macroeconomic stability, characterized by a favourable inflation rate, a steadily increasing gross domestic product as well as increasing rates of savings and investments. Furthermore, it was noted that political stability is a precondition for macroeconomic stability.

2. A microfinance programme by itself is not sufficient for poverty alleviation. Such programmes should be complemented by technical extension services, training and marketing assistance in activities connected to the loans. Credit should be extended for income-generating activities in which the borrowers have had previous experience. Furthermore, women should be involved at all stages of the design and implementation of microfinance programmes designed for them.

3. In the case of small loans, it may not be necessary to include physical collateral among the criteria for determining creditworthiness. However, physical collateral may be required for loans which are large. In the case of loans extended through a group-as-collateral system, the group should be recognized as a legal entity. In order to ensure accountability in cases of loan defaults, the group should be registered by the relevant authorities. Furthermore, financial intermediaries may be regulated by banking laws in certain countries.

4. The establishment of additional financial institutions creates competition and permits greater choice for borrowers. Such institutions should avoid duplication of activities and must be regulated by an external supervisory agency.

5. To remove existing sociocultural barriers, including biases against women, a government should take the initiative in formulating anti-discriminatory policies and programmes.

6. To ensure that the financial institutions regard women as being creditworthy, universal education programmes which promote literacy and numeracy should be implemented. Administrative procedures required by the financial institutions should be simplified in order to make them comprehensible to the borrowers. Parallel to the procedural simplification, training for bank staff should incorporate topics intended to increase understanding of the needs of women borrowers.

7. To promote awareness of the objectives, procedures and processes of formal financial institutions, information campaigns through the media and other means should be utilized.

8.	In order to facilitate access to formal financial institutions, the physical infra-structure of such institutions should be improved. Service units or transaction offices should be established in remote areas where full branch offices are not viable.	Outreach to the door-step of targeted beneficiaries should be extended through mobile banking in areas with poor transport connections.	To increase the impression of accessibility to the formal financial institutions, bank premises and facilities should be made more accommodating.

9.	With regard to the interest rate policy, it was noted that certain countries used the market rate of interest in order to assure the long-term sustainability of formal financial institutions. In some countries, lower-than-market interest rates existed. It was recommended that interest rate policies should be guided by the costs of operations, loan losses, inflation and funds.

10.	Donor agencies should recognize the importance of microcredit programmes, especially those which address the needs of women.	During the developmental stages of the formal financial institutions, donor support or subsidy to cover the social mobilization and initial investment costs may be required.	In the long term, donor dependency should be reduced.

11.	Prudential guidelines should take into consideration the special circumstances of the financial institutions catering to the needs of the non-traditional borrowers. In order to promote the integration of non-traditional borrowers into the formal financial sector, financial institutions should be given more flexibility in their mandates and functions, i.e., in terms of client choice, loan purposes and conditions for loans. Institutional capacity may need further strengthening.

12.	The relationship between the financial institution and the client requires a linkage between savings and credit. Savings mobilization leads to a larger stock of capital available to borrowers and to the self-sustainability of the financial institution. Savings can be used as collateral, a precondition for granting loans and a reserve for emergencies.	Innovative savings products should also be introduced to motivate women and acquaint them with saving habits and banking activities. A reasonable rate of return and savings collection services at the local level should be ensured.

13.	Group savings funds derived from voluntary and compulsory savings may be used by members for meeting emergencies, certain consumption needs or social functions, as well as for productive uses.

14.	In order to address the high level of administrative costs relative to loan size and the use of the group-as-collateral method, intermediaries such as non-governmental and mass organizations may be used.	Such intermediaries can reduce the transaction costs as well as assure repayment.

15.	A coordination mechanism among donor agencies, formal financial institutions, non-governmental or mass organizations, and client groups is a necessary criterion for increasing the effectiveness of programmes targeted towards women within a country.

16.   In line with the declaration of the 1997 Micro Credit Summit, it was recommended that participating countries should formulate national targets for reaching poor families, and particularly women, by 2005. Policies should be implemented in order to reach the national targets.

17.   In order to promote the exchange of ideas and experiences, the possibilities for coordination among formal financial institutions in participating countries should be explored. In that regard, it may be useful to designate a focal point in each country and establish a forum to facilitate related follow-up activities.

PART TWO

POLICIES AND PRACTICES OF SELECTED FORMAL CREDIT AND FINANCIAL INSTITUTIONS IN THE ASIA-PACIFIC REGION[1]

Introduction

Formal financial institutions have often been inaccessible to both women and the poor. Since the poor are often illiterate and cannot provide collateral in the form of a title to an asset, usually land, formal financial institutions have often presumed that the poor are non-bankable. The requirement for physical collateral by those financial institutions has likewise excluded many women from undertaking transactions in the formal financial sector.

Given the reluctance of formal financial institutions to fulfill the credit and savings requirements of women, two modalities in microfinance have evolved during the past two decades. The first modality developed through the establishment of financial institutions that specifically serve the financial needs of the poor. Notable examples of such institutions are the Grameen Bank of Bangladesh, the Self-Employed Women's Association (SEWA), Bank of India, First Women's Bank of Pakistan and the Vietnam Bank for the Poor. The second evolved through the re-examination of established formal financial institutions and modification of their practices in order to improve access to less-traditional borrowers. Examples include government-initiated credit programmes administered through State-owned banks such as Indonesia's Income Generating Project for Marginal Farmers and Landless (P4K), implemented by the government's agricultural extension service and the Bank Rakyat Indonesia (BRI), and the Small Farmers Development Programme (SFDP), undertaken by the Agricultural Development Bank of Nepal (ADBN).

These microfinance modalities have shown that it is possible to bank with the poor, and in particular, with poor women. However, the capability of such institutions to reach large numbers of non-traditional borrowers is still limited. In addition, there is no concrete evidence that the polices and practices implemented by formal financial institutions actually provided women or the poor with easier access.

---

[1] Based on a paper prepared by Generoso G. Octavio, consultant, for presentation at the Regional Seminar on Improving the Access of Women to Formal Credit and Financial Institutions, Hanoi, Viet Nam, 1-4 July 1997.

The study on Viet Nam reproduced in the next chapter indicates that "in comparison with men, women find it more difficult to borrow".[2] Even when a loan application is approved, the loan proceeds are not disbursed as expected and women borrowers obtain only 50 per cent of their required loan amount. Moreover, key formal financial institutions serve wealthier women who are able to provide collateral for loans while the newly-established Vietnam Bank for the Poor serves very poor households. Private moneylenders charge high interest rates on loans to the majority of women borrowers who fall between categories of wealth and poor. A survey in 1994, for example, showed that the formal banking sector provided only 30 per cent of total loans and that the informal credit sector provided the remaining 70 per cent. Another survey conducted by the Viet Nam General Statistics Office in the same year revealed that only 20 per cent of total available loans were taken out by female-headed households.

To work effectively, lending policies and practices aimed at enhancing the access of women to formal credit require a thorough understanding of their needs. Only then will existing formal financial institutions be able to identify and amend their weaknesses, reduce constraints faced by women in dealing with those institutions, and firmly integrate women borrowers into the formal financial sector.

Section A of this chapter provides a general overview of the current policies and practices by formal and semi-formal microfinance institutions, as well as formal sector banks with microfinance programmes, undertaken in collaboration with government agencies and non-governmental organizations.[3]

Section B presents major policies, procedures and practices on poverty and gender-focused lending by formal financial institutions in selected developing and least developed countries in Asia.[4] It includes recent developments on lending and saving policies and practices in a number of those countries which were discussed during the Regional Seminar on Improving the Access of Women to Formal Credit and Financial Institutions, held from 1 to 4 July 1997 in Hanoi. The section also discusses government policy initiatives to improve access by women to formal credit, as well as practices by semi-formal and informal institutions that merit adoption by the formal financial sector.

Section C enumerates a set of recommendations related to policies and practices which governments and institutions can implement to improve access by women to formal credit and financial institutions.

---

[2] Phan Ke Hoang, *Improving the Access of Women to Formal Credit and Financial Institutions in Selected Least-Developed Countries of the Asian and Pacific Region: Viet Nam* (Hanoi, Vietnam Bank for Agriculture and Rural Development, April 1997), p. 18.

[3] A formal credit institution is loosely defined as one which is under the control and supervision of the central bank and which follows conventional banking rules and regulations set forth in its charter. A semi-formal financial institution is usually not regulated by the central bank. Non-governmental organizations (NGOs) may exclusively or as a component undertake financial activities among their clients or beneficiaries.

[4] See *Improving the Access of Women to Formal Credit and Financial Institutions: Windows of Opportunity* (ST/ESCAP/1601).

A. Overview of policies and practices

Many policies to improve access to formal and semi-formal financial institutions by women have evolved over the past 20 years. The inability of the formal financial sector to address the micro-financial requirements of women and the poor, and the failure of farmers' credit programmes which offered agricultural credit tied to inputs during the Green Revolution, spurred the development of alternatives. Focus also shifted towards gender-sensitive issues and programmes which would increase the participation of women in social and economic development. Many of those programmes focused on improving access to productive resources, of which credit was one critical factor.

1. Cost reduction

The large number of potential women borrowers, the micro nature of their income-generating activities, and their need for small loans imply high administrative costs. Joint liability groups have been established as a means of reducing transaction costs both for lenders and borrowers, as well as reducing administrative and default costs. In a joint liability group, its officers apply for a single wholesale loan from a financial institution which is then retailed to individual members. Time-consuming loan paper work and credit investigation necessary for individual loans are drastically minimized as the group is liable for the entire loan. The bank or intermediary institution conducts transactions only with one or two of the group officers who use a single loan application. Through joint liability groups, each credit officer at a financial institution is able to serve more clients in a given period of time. Members of the group do not need to incur transportation costs or other opportunity expenses in connection with the loan approval process. Furthermore, group dynamics and peer pressure are more effective in ensuring better repayment by borrowers.

2. Use of non-physical collateral

Physical collateral as a requirement for conventional loans has prevented the majority of the poor and women from gaining access to credit. Without land title deeds or property than can be mortgaged, the poor are not able to borrow from a bank. The same holds true for women who are not signatories to land title deeds or who have lost their inheritance of land to male household members. Widowed, separated, divorced and abandoned women who have lost their property rights are the most affected by the requirement among formal banks for physical collateral.

(a) *Group collateral*

For those who cannot provide physical collateral, borrowing through a joint liability group offers an effective alternative to the traditional modalities of lending. A joint liability group can assess the feasibility of a loan application, consider the practical uses for the loan and determine the terms of repayment. Physical collateral is not necessary as long as a client is a member of the group which approves the loan application.   In addition to group formation and membership, a group culture that is characterized by credit discipline and mutual concern among its members needs to be maintained.   Such characteristics enable the group to be a sound alternative to the physical collateral required by formal financial institutions.

The group-as-collateral policy has been almost universally applied in micro-finance programmes undertaken by governments and the formal banking sector. Similarly, microfinance institutions (MFIs) which had initially experimented with lending through groups have now fully adopted, and are aggressively promoting, the group-as-collateral policy in lieu of conventional physical collateral.

The status of a group applying for formal and semi-formal loans using the group-as-collateral approach has been raised as a legal issue.   The issue centres upon whom to hold accountable for funds which have been borrowed by the group but have not been repaid. Although individuals who fail to make repayments on their loans can be prosecuted, the procedure for holding absconding groups responsible remains unclear.

Box II.1. Use of group-as-collateral in microfinance programmes

Microfinance programmes operated by government-owned and controlled banks and private commercial banks, as well as specialized microfinance institutions serving poor women borrowers, have used the group-as-collateral approach to circumvent the physical collateral requirement.

In the Philippines, the Bank of Philippine Islands (BPI), a large and well-established private commercial bank, has been supporting non-governmental organization (NGO) and cooperative microfinance projects through its social development arm, the BPI Foundation. The NGOs use the group-as-collateral approach for loans from BPI which are on-lent mostly to poor women and small enterprises. One NGO that has an indirect credit line with the bank is Ahon Sa Hirap, Inc (ASHI), a university-based action-research project funded by the United Nations Development Programme (UNDP) through the Asia and Pacific Development Centre which replicated the Grameen Bank approach in 1989. ASHI clients are all very poor women whose initial loans averaged only US$ 40 per borrower. It features group formation, weekly meetings to collect small savings and repayment amortization, interest on loans at the market rate, simple lending procedures, close supervision, rigorous training of staff and clients, efficient financial management and record-keeping. Clients receive loans on the basis of group approval to ensure proper loan use and repayment. Risk is minimized by a reserve against loan loss established through the group savings fund. Collective savings of group members are used to cover the unpaid principal or interest resulting from difficulty in repayment by any of its members.

Other notable examples of microfinance institutions using this approach are the Grameen Bank and the Association for Social Advancement (ASA) in Bangladesh, Grameen Bikash Bank in Nepal, Association of Cambodian Local Economic Development Agencies (ACLEDA) in Cambodia, the Self-Employed Women's Association (SEWA), Bank of India, Amanah Ikhtiar Malaysia (AIM) and the Vietnam Bank for the Poor (VBP). Other institutions in the region employ the "credit plus" approach which incorporates the provision of credit along with other social development activities.

(b) *Modified collateral policy*

Some government-owned and controlled banks have modified their collateral policy to improve access by the poor and women to their credit resources. The collateral requirement, for example, can be waived for certain sizes of loan. The Vietnam Bank for the Poor has removed the physical collateral requirement for loans of dong 2.5 million (approximately US$ 200) or less. Even if physical collateral is required, banks may also consider equipment or machinery rather than a land title as a guarantee against the loan. Guarantors, promissory notes and guaranteed funds may also replace physical collateral.

3. Interest rate policy

The viability and sustainability of formal financial institutions depend on their operational and financial self-sufficiency. The policy for setting the interest rate on loans is guided by: (a) the cost of operations; (b) cost of default; (c) opportunity cost of equity capital; (d) cost of debt capital; and (e) inflation cost.

Formal financial institutions such as commercial banks usually charge market-determined interest. Agricultural and rural development banks may charge lower-than-market rates of interest for certain loans, including those meant for long-term development projects. Rates may also differ slightly for clients in rural and urban areas.

It has been asserted that women and the poor should obtain loans at interest rates lower than the market rate. It has also been argued, however, that the poor and especially women borrowers can repay loans at market or even higher-than-market interest rates. Evidence from Indonesia (P4K), Bangladesh (Grameen Bank), Philippines (among Grameen Bank approach replicators), and Viet Nam (IFAD-supported credit projects through the Vietnam Bank for the Poor) support this view. Private money lenders have proliferated in poorer countries where the formal financial system is not well-developed. Although the interest rate they charge is high, their activities continue, indicating that access to credit, rather than the interest rate itself, is the constraint limiting the success of microfinance programmes.

4. Social mobilization subsidy

A subsidy on the costs of social mobilization and the training of poor and mostly illiterate women is necessary for implementing a successful microfinance programme. A subsidy on the initial costs of establishing a microfinance institution or programme can also be required. To promote institutional sustainability and self-reliance, the subsidy and donor assistance should be gradually withdrawn after the developmental stage. Microfinance institutions like the Grameen Bank and ASA, and microfinance programmes like P4K are either moving towards or are already at that stage. The capability of the institution to maintain microfinance activities through a regime of non-subsidized costs, market rate of interest and efficient savings mobilization is a necessary condition for their long-run sustainability.

5. Links and coordination

To make their loan funds more accessible to a large number of women clients, formal commercial and development banks should establish links with microfinance institutions, non-governmental organizations, self-help groups and mass organizations like the Women's Unions in Cambodia, the Lao People's Democratic Republic and Viet Nam. The establishment of links between those institutions will enable them to exploit their comparative advantages. Banks have credit funds but are constrained from lending to clients who cannot fulfill their collateral requirements. Microfinance institutions, non-governmental organizations and other institutions have the capability to mobilize, organize and train borrowers, but they are constrained by the lack of funds both for the initial development outlay and potential loans. By complementing each institution's strengths and available resources, it is possible to overcome formal sector impediments such as complicated lending procedures and stringent loan application requirements, as well as client-based constraints including illiteracy, lack of credit information and geographical barriers. The intermediary organizations thus assist in removing those obstacles for the women clients and the formal credit source.

Banks can provide credit to poor women borrowers through indirect links through intermediaries and through direct links through joint liability groups. In the former case, the intermediary borrows from the participating bank at a low rate of interest. The funds are then lent by the intermediary to its members. In the latter case, borrowers acquire their loans directly from the bank, but only the officers of the group actually deal with the bank. In both cases, the group serves as the collateral for formal credit.

Coordination among government agencies, banks and intermediary organiza-tions have emerged as an issue due to the proliferation of microfinance programmes run by governments, NGOs and semi-formal financial institutions. In certain countries, NGOs with similar mandates and credit delivery mechanisms operate within the same geographical locations, causing duplication of activities, poor resource allocation and confusion among borrowers as a result of different interest rates and conditions for similar types of loans and groups of borrowers.

6. Linked savings and credit policy

The generation of savings has been an important component of successful credit programmes. Micro-credit programmes which were initially implemented in Bangladesh, India, Nepal and Pakistan relied heavily on small savings which were compulsory and regularly collected from borrowers.

In the South-East Asia, the P4K programme of BRI has generated savings from its small borrowers. Likewise in the Philippines, microfinance and semi-formal financial institutions, in partnership with the Land Bank of the Philippines and other private development banks, have followed the policy of linked savings and credit. Under that policy, a client is not allowed to borrow through the group unless a certain amount has been already saved. The Bank for Agriculture and Agricultural Cooperatives (BAAC) in Thailand relies on savings mobilization to raise its credit delivery to small farmers and it promotes a habit of saving among women farmers. In Malaysia, the government supports financial assistance to the *bumiputras* or indigenous Malays through the Grameen-type microfinance institution, AIM, which has a savings mobilization scheme among its mostly poor women borrowers.

In countries of the region which have had closed economies and relatively undeveloped financial systems, informal rotating savings and credit groups, more commonly known as "village revolving funds", are practised. Such schemes are common among women in remote rural areas where formal banks are absent. No one in the group can borrow unless a small contribution to the group fund has been made prior to borrowing. Once the first loan has been repaid, other members in the circle can borrow. The scheme can be modified so that the amount of loan that a member is entitled to borrow depends on the amount of savings that the individual had already contributed. Since the members collectively formulate and adopt the conditions for lending on a case-by-case basis, the interest rate and terms of repayment for each loan may vary.

7. Participatory planning

A programme or project targeted at women tends to succeed when they are allowed to directly participate in the development process. Women want to participate in policy formulation, programme planning and direct implementation of projects that are meant for them. Experiences of successful microfinance institutions in South Asia have shown that women have the capacity to organize, and participate in, activities that concern them. In practice, most of the successful strategies have been designed and tested by the target beneficiaries themselves.

Microfinance institutions like the Grameen Bank have emphasized that women should be allowed to form groups by themselves. This process of self-selection or self-group formation promptly eliminates institutional problems that may arise in the future. For example, group failure may be blamed on the bank if the bank worker had chosen and grouped the members, rather than the members grouping by themselves. Moreover, villagers have better knowledge of those who are good borrowers and will make use of loan proceeds wisely. Thus, even at that stage of the microfinance scheme, peer group pressure, credit discipline and good repayment are already encouraged. This process ensures successful programme implementation and institution-building with the targeted clientele, and provides lessons for government policy makers and the formal banking sector.

B. Recent developments in microfinance policies and practices

Using two well-known linkage experiments implemented in Indonesia, namely, P4K and Linking Banks and Self-Help Groups Project (PHBK), this section illustrates how policies which have been formulated for the poor and translated into workable practices can improve the access by women to the formal financial services. The former is a joint project between BRI and the Ministry of Agriculture, while the latter is a collaborative project between Bank Indonesia and the German aid agency, GTZ. Both aim to make formal financial services and resources accessible to the lower income group of borrowers through institutional links and the use of group mechanism. A third modality is illustrated by the case of the Grameen Bank of Bangladesh.

The second part of this section narrates some recent developments in microfinance policies and practices which enhance the access by women to both formal and semi-formal credit. Experiences in the countries discussed during the Regional Seminar on Improving the Access of Women to Formal Credit and Financial Institutions have also been incorporated.

1. A formal bank's innovation: P4K programme of Bank Rakyat Indonesia

(a) *Practices and policies*

BRI presents an example of a formal financial institution with a well-formulated set of policies and sound practices to provide formal credit to poor households, including those headed by women. As a general policy, the Government of Indonesian has targeted all microenterprises for its action-oriented credit and savings programmes. Other policy guidelines include: (a) the development of financial programmes for microenterprises along commercial lines; (b) the utilization of existing organizational and institutional resources; (c) the establishment of a financial intermediation system that links formal financial institutions with semi-formal (self-help promoting institution) and informal (self-help groups) institutions; and (d) a combination of savings mobilization and credit delivery schemes in the programmes.

Financial institutions for the poor and women, which would be an alternative to the existing formal banks, have not been created in Indonesia. To enable credit to flow from formal institutions to clients who are organized in self-help or mutual aid groups, existing formal, semi-formal and informal institutions are used instead. Consistent with their policy on commercialized lending, the interest rates charged on loans are either market rates or possibly even higher. For example, a scheme with the Cooperative Bank of Indonesia provides market-priced banking services through multipurpose rural cooperatives to borrowers at the village level. Loans from the Cooperative Bank are charged an annual 18 per cent interest. The funds are on-lent to members of multipurpose cooperatives at an annual interest rate of 48 per cent. Of the 30 per cent interest spread, 6 per cent is distributed as management fees for staff of the two cooperatives, 6 per cent covers overhead costs and 18 per cent becomes the group profit.

(b) *Practices and schemes*

Project P4K has six operating guidelines: (a) a group lending approach; (b) homogeneity within the groups; (c) the development of leadership; (d) self-reliance; (e) learning by doing; and (f) a total family approach. It has three key strategies: (a) human development; (b) financial accessibility; and (c) institution-building. These strategies are implemented through three main areas of activities: (a) the development of small farmer groups; (b) the provision of necessary extension support and training to enable clients to operate small business enterprises, and (c) the provision of credit from the formal banking sector to finance rural income-generating enterprises.

Procedural steps in operation include: (a) identification of project location and resource potential using small business and location surveys; (b) the formation of self-help groups among low-income families after a household survey of potential group members; (c) assistance to clients in group business planning, loan application and the generation of savings; (d) training and assistance in the implementation of the business plan, simple accounting and bookkeeping, marketing, and capital accumulation and re-investment; and (e) training of farm extension workers and senior field extension workers.

The P4K project proved that the poor could be integrated into the formal banking system and that, in collaboration with the government extension agency, formal financial institutions could be an effective tool for poverty alleviation. It also proved that it was possible to lend to the poor without requiring collateral while still generating an adequate profit for sustainability. That experience demonstrates a helpful lesson for governments searching for a methodology that uses existing institutions for poverty reduction, rather than establishing alternative banking institutions which would cater to less traditional borrowers.

2. PHBK, a central bank's initiative: linking banks with self-help groups

In 1988 Bank Indonesia, with assistance from GTZ, initiated the first pilot project linking banks with self-help groups, thereby establishing linkages among participating banks, self-help promoting institutions (SHPIs) and self-help groups (SHGs). This led to the establishment of the first Bank-SHG linkage in Yogyakarta, Indonesia, on 31 May 1989. The financial sector deregulation which coincided with the launch of the project furthermore created a "favourable environment for the linkage project".[5]

---

[5] *PHBK: The Indonesian Linkage Project (Brief Expose on Strategy and Performance)* (Jakarta, UKK-PHBK Bank Indonesia, September 1996), p. 4.

(a) *Principles and policies*

Given the changes in the financial sector, the guiding principles of PHBK were as follows:[6]

    (a)   Apply a group approach to providing financial services to micro-entrepreneurs and small farmers who have no access to the formal banking sector;

    (b)   Select participating institutions carefully by checking eligibility;

    (c)   Respect the autonomy of participating institutions;

    (d)   Promote savings mobilization among SHGs through the formal banking sector, and linking savings with credit;

    (e)   Achieve financial viability by applying market interest rates to savings and credit, covering transaction costs from interest margins;

    (f)   Supplement traditional physical collateral with alternative collateral such as group liability and blocked savings;

    (g)   Concentrate on linkage partners that promise the highest degree of sustainability and coverage.

(b) *Practices and schemes*

The PHBK project enhanced the "bankability" of each group through guidance and training to improve organizational skills, bookkeeping and financial management. PHBK acted as a motivator and facilitator of linkages, while SHPI were responsible for upgrading savings and credit groups into bankable groups, and for facilitating financial linkages with banks.

The PHBK scheme consists of a one-week training-of-trainers course for SHPI staff on how to train credit and savings groups in financial management. Bank staff are encouraged to attend the course so they can become familiar with the process of improving the bankability of credit and savings groups. The second step involves identification of eligible credit and savings groups by SHPI for participation in the PHBK training course according to PHBK eligibility criteria. As the third step, members of eligible credit and savings groups receive a one-week PHBK financial management training course with guidance from SHPI staff. Finally, SHPI facilitates financial links between banks and qualified credit and savings groups. The credit and savings groups then transfer savings from the group fund to the bank to serve as collateral. The credit and savings groups, in turn, obtain refinancing credit from the bank. The maximum amount of refinancing credit is calculated by a savings-credit ratio determined by the bank. Guidance by SHPI, to ensure regular loan repayments to the bank, continues even after the linkage with the bank has been formed.

---

[6]   Ibid.

3. Specialized microfinance innovation: Grameen Bank

(a) *Policies and principles*

The Grameen Bank of Bangladesh has different financial policies and principles for developing a poverty-focused financial system. Those principles include: (a) direct targeting of poorest households; (b) a focus on women as clients; (c) non-collateral lending through group formation; (d) banking on existing or "native" skills of borrowers; (e) maintaining transparency in all transactions; (f) establishing a market rate of interest orientation; (g) maintaining an innovative approach to savings mobilization and deposit generation programmes; and (h) aiming for viability and sustainability.

Before the Grameen Bank became an institutionalized bank, it operated as a window for an existing formal bank. To serve the financial needs of the rural communities, the Grameen Bank developed its doorstep credit delivery programme, under which bank workers went directly to the villages rather than requiring the borrowers to go to banks located in towns. The programme also incorporated intensive training for clients and bank staff. The large number of qualified borrowers in the programme required the formation of groups to permit cost-effective and systematic credit delivery and recovery.

A distinct philosophy and a targeted clientele called for a banking strategy which included social mobilization, motivation and training of clients, and basic financial accounting. The Grameen Bank was therefore transformed from a window for a formal bank to an autonomous bank specializing in non-conventional banking with the poor. The bank charges market interest rates for small initial loans. Over the years, its loan recovery rates have been close to 100 per cent and the Grameen Bank figures prominently as a pioneer microfinance institution that offers alternative banking for the poorest households. Table II.1 lists the principles and policies adopted by BRI and the Grameen Bank.

Table II.1. Lending and saving principles and policies of formal financial institutions: Bank Rakyat Indonesia and Grameen Bank

Bank Rakyat Indonesia (Formal State commercial bank)	Grameen Bank (Alternative specialized bank)
Market rate of interest	Market rate of interest
Group-as-collateral (non-collateral lending)	Group-as-collateral (non-collateral lending)
Linking self-help groups with formal sector	Direct focus on the poorest
Use of existing organizational and institutional resources	Targeting on women as borrowers
Targeting both formal and informal sector borrowers	Intensive staff and client training
Training on technical and financial skills	Banking on existing skills of the poor
Savings mobilization combined with credit delivery mobilization	Transparency in all transactions
Sustainability through savings	Compulsory and voluntary savings
	Aiming at visibility and sustainability

(b) *Procedures and practices*

The establishment of the Grameen Bank resulted from a series of field-based experiments in village banking with the poor. Its methodology was developed primarily for poor women who were employed both in household and micro-business activities in their homes and farms. To ensure that loans reach the target, credit is directly delivered to villages. Potential borrowers are identified through village surveys and motivated to form groups through self-selected group formation. They are trained to understand the rules and their responsibilities. Bank staff are also trained intensively, both on existing banking methodology and on innovative banking for the poor.

Savings are mobilized on a weekly basis in small amounts. Loans are prepared using simple documentation, and the initial loan is small. Repayments are made on a weekly basis in small amounts to enable clients to repay. Credit discipline is instilled through regular attendance at weekly meetings and peer or group pressure which holds each member responsible for the proper utilization and recovery of loans.

The methodology developed by the Grameen Bank has become the pattern for group-based financial services and has been widely adopted, adapted and replicated. The International Fund for Agricultural Development (IFAD), which supported the Grameen Bank in its early years, has tried to channel institutional credit to the rural poor through rural finance interventions. Its basic methodology seeks to: (a) identify beneficiaries/clients; (b) encourage group formation on the basis of self-selection; (c) initiate group savings activities; (d) develop group cohesion and peer pressure mechanism; (e) develop links with the credit agencies; (f) obtain credit; (g) undertake income-generating activities; and (h) repay the loans.[7] Quasi- and semi-formal financial organizations, including international and local NGOs, have also learned a number of lessons from the Grameen Bank approach.

4. Recent developments in microfinance in least developed countries

This subsection draws on the sharing of experiences among countries in the region which were represented during the Regional Seminar on Improving the Access of Women to Formal Credit and Financial Institutions, as well as countries in the original study. Recent policy instruments and practices presented by each country are also summarized.

(a) *Bangladesh*

The central bank promotes a policy of formal sector support to microfinance institutions through the linkage mechanism. ASA, one of the fastest-growing microfinance institutions in Bangladesh, recently received loans from the formal

---

[7] "Micro-Finance in IFAD-Funded Projects: Lessons Learned and Emerging Issues" (Kuala Lumpur, UNOPS Asia Office, March 1997), p. 1.

banking sector for lending in certain geographical locations.[8]   For example, ASA has negotiated a loan of Tk 44 million at an annual interest rate of 9 per cent and it has already drawn Tk 10 million from Agrani Bank, one of three government-owned banks in Bangladesh.   ASA has also borrowed funds for on-lending from the Bank for Small Industries and Commerce (BASIC Bank) at an annual interest rate of 7 per cent.

Loans for the poor can also be acquired from international funding agencies through local development finance institutions.   In its bid to expand credit operations, ASA has finalized a loan of US$ 20 million from IDA-World Bank through the Palli Karma Shahayak Foundation (PKSF).   The foundation provides loans to poverty alleviation programmes at an annual interest rate of 4.5 per cent.   ASA has acquired operational and managerial skills to handle larger amounts of funds for income-generating activities by its client groups and for expansion.[9]

Since they comprise institutional policies for ensuring sustainable credit for poor women, microfinance institutions such as ASA do not require collateral for loans, while running operations from income, and effectively mobilizing savings. Microfinance practices usually include: a group-based lending approach with 20-25 members per group; small, compulsory weekly savings; training on habitual savings and credit awareness; small initial loan sizes of Tk 3,000-7,000; weekly instalment payments of the loan principal; minimal administrative expenses; 1 per cent of provision loan disbursed to an insurance fund; simplified record keeping; fast loan processing (two weeks from loan application to disbursement); decentralized management; and active participation by women members.[10]

(b) *Bhutan*

Bhutan has yet to formulate clear gender sensitive policies aimed at improving access by women to formal credit.   Due to the failure of the individual lending system, the high cost of credit operations and low recovery rates, the Bhutan Development Finance Corporation (BDFC) has proposed a pragmatic modality for enhancing the microcredit delivery system.

Under this new modality, rural clients form self-help groups with 5 to 10 members each.   Credit will be provided to self-help groups and their members on the basis of a group guarantee lending system.   The group guarantee lending system was selected because it permitted: (a) proper identification of clients; (b) sound appraisal of

---

8   *ASA Sustainable Micro-Finance Model* (Dhaka, Association for Social Advancement, July 1996), p. 7.

9   Ibid.

10 The Association for Social Advancement's "self-reliant development model" is implemented in the field by a unit office, which comprises one unit manager, four community organizers (COs) and one service staff member.   A unit office is managerially responsible to about 1,240 to 1,440 members (mostly women).   The CO collects weekly savings and loan principal instalments with assistance from the group chairman and treasurer. The unit manager approves and disburses loans. Daily cash collections can be disbursed as loans on the same day.   Loan amortization is standardized for easy and quick record keeping.   The unit office maintains the loan ledgers and cash books.

loan requests by SHG members; (c) correct assessment of the repayment capacity of SHG members; (d) proper utilization of the loan proceeds; (e) effective monitoring, supervision and evaluation of project implementation; (f) timely repayment of loan instalments; (g) a collective guarantee for loan repayments; and (h) an absence of security for individual SHG members to pledge.[11]

Decentralization of microcredit services to cover all regions of the country is an overriding government policy. With the participation of the National Women's Association of Bhutan (NWAB), outreach to women microentrepreneurs and farmers is expected to improve.

(c) *Cambodia*

In Cambodia, the formal financial system remains undeveloped. Since rural banks are non-existent, the demand for credit by poor women is met by local and international NGOs. Among the leading local NGOs, the most extensive national coverage is provided by ACLEDA, which focuses on the provision of sustainable and demand-driven financial and business development services to rural poor women.

As a member of the Credit Committee for Rural Development (CCRD), ACLEDA collaborates closely with the Ministry of Women's Affairs at the national level and the Women in Development programmes at the provincial level. Women clients receive assistance not only in credit extension but also in terms of access to technical skills, business advice and market information. Policies are set and loan procedures are designed for the benefit of women. Women can easily apply for and receive loan disbursements from ACLEDA. Moreover, women receive loan allocation priority.

ACLEDA practices typical village banking strategies such as disbursing small loan amounts in the first cycles, non-collateralized group loans, savings mobilization and non-subsidized interest rates. The loan procedure for group lending comprises: (a) area identification; (b) community meetings; (c) group formation; (d) information collection and assessment through a baseline survey; (e) provision of basic microbusiness management training; (f) loan document preparation; (g) loan application approval; and (h) loan disbursement.

The achievements of ACLEDA as a microfinance institution in Cambodia can be further enhanced by ensuring a favourable and stable socio-economic and political environment. ACLEDA provides policy makers and the formal banking regulatory body with experiences in microfinance for improving access by women. Plans are being formulated for transforming ACLEDA into a bank or a formal microfinance institution.

---

[11] "A Brief Note on Enhancement of Microcredit Delivery System in Bhutan". Paper presented at the Regional Seminar on Improving Access of Women to Formal Credit, Hanoi, Viet Nam, 1-4 July 1997.

(d) *Lao People's Democratic Republic*

Women in the Lao People's Democratic Republic are supposed to have access to loans from formal sources which is equal to that enjoyed by men. The proportion of women making use of banking services, however, is much lower than the proportion of women who borrow from semi-formal and informal sources. With the exception of the credit and savings activities of the Lao Women's Union, a leading mass organization, women have minimal access to formal financial institutions. Banking services in rural areas are more limited than in peri-urban areas. However, as a result of reforms in the financial system, the Agricultural Promotion Bank will expand to reach more small farmers and rural dwellers.

The Lao People's Democratic Republic has yet to implement measures for developing microfinance institutions which offer financial services to women. Traders who usually provide in-kind loans and marketing services are currently financing women's productive activities such as weaving. The arrangement, however, does not guarantee fair prices for the products.

Current policies of the Agricultural Promotion Bank do not include charging a market rate of interest on loans to farmer. The Lang Xang Bank, a commercial bank based in the rural areas, offers market rate loans but also requires physical collateral. Most of its clients are not poor but are women from more affluent households in the provinces who can provide collateral. The Lang Xang Bank and Agricultural Promotion Bank, however, can deal with clients through village headmen and credit-savings agents who represent groups of village borrowers.

A plethora of village revolving funds (VRFs) has been implemented by international NGOs which are operating in the country. Most VRFs involve cash and in-kind lending to poor small farmers in the countryside. Through external seed capital, villagers establish so-called "animal banks" and "rice banks", along with village banks that lend and recover cash. The Lao Women's Union also manages and coordinates revolving funds for women in rural areas

It appears that a semi-formal credit and savings arrangements may be the "most appropriate and successful in reaching disadvantaged and resource-poor communities and groups in rural Lao People's Democratic Republic, many of whom would not otherwise have any access to credit".[12] Those arrangements are characterized by: (a) suitability to local conditions and realities; (b) relatively small loan sizes; (c) group responsibility and guarantees in lieu of collateral; (d) strong technical back-up through training and monitoring; (e) strong community institutions; and (f) participation both by women and men in management and decision-making.

To promote microfinance principles and practices, together with the development of a sustainable microfinance system, the Government of the Lao People's Democratic Republic, UNDP and the United Nations Capital Development Fund

---

[12] Country report presented by the Lao Women's Union at the Regional Seminar on Improving the Access of Women to Formal Credit and Financial Institutions, Hanoi, Viet Nam, 1-4 July 1997.

(UNCDF) will undertake a national project on microfinance over the next five years. The project includes the formulation of a legal framework under which microfinance institutions could operate, including the preparation of regulations on non-bank financial institutions. Those microfinance institutions established, strengthened or expanded through the project will extend micro-loans and savings services to an increasing number of women.

(e) *Myanmar*

The Myanma Agricultural Development Bank (MADB), the only State-owned bank that provides seasonal, short-term and long-term credit to farmers in Myanmar, has over two million clients. The bank finances agricultural, livestock breeding and rural socio-economic projects. Since overall government lending policy is non-sex discriminatory, women and men should have equal opportunity when accessing loans from formal financial institutions in Myanmar.

MADB has grassroots organizations called villager banks which increase outreach and serve as basic units for channelling agricultural credit to farmers. A total of 12,280 villager banks have been formed. Membership in a villager bank is voluntary and without gender bias, but the applicant must be a household head.[13] Members must purchase shares of 10 kyats each upon admission to membership. Lending and accounting functions of the villager banks are undertaken by elected committee members under the supervision of MADB branches. Loan viability and repayment capacity of each applicant are the main criteria for approving a term loan. Since seasonal loans are disbursed by the villager banks based on joint liability, no physical collateral is required.

The Central Bank of Myanmar provides loan funds to MADB at a 1 per cent nominal service charge. MADB makes loans to villager banks at an annual interest rate of 13 per cent. The villager banks on-lend to members at 15 per cent. The 2 per cent margin is deposited by villager banks in a profit savings account with a MADB branch or agency. The profit covers loan handling, collection and management expenses, as well as travel and subsistence allowances for committee members of villager banks.

Savings are mobilized by compelling each farmer-borrower to deposit 1 per cent of his/her loan principal repayment into a compulsory savings account. A rural savings programme was launched to mobilize deposits of surplus income by farmers and other members of the rural population. A 12 per cent interest on savings deposits is given and depositors may take out development loans of up to four or five times the amount of their deposits, at an annual interest rate of 15 per cent. Late repayment of loans is penalized by 1 per cent interest. The recovery rate of villager bank loans has so far been almost 100 per cent.

---

[13] Taken from notes on "Improving the Access of Women to Formal Credit and Financial Institutions in Myanmar". Presented at the Regional Seminar on Improving Access of Women to Formal Credit, Hanoi, Viet Nam, 1-4 July 1997.

(f) *Nepal*

Nepal has implemented a number of steps to increase opportunities for women to access formal credit. Specific policy measures have resulted in the establishment of the projects and programmes detailed below.

(i) *Women Small Farmers Development Project*

The Women Small Farmers Development Project (WSFDP) project, which is wholly operated by women staff, targets rural women. It follows the philosophy of the Small Farmers Development Programme (SFDP), a project of the Agricultural Development ment Bank of Nepal (ADBN). Basic features of WSFDP include collateral-free, short-term loans, manageable group size, use of loans for both farm and non-farm income generating activities, negotiable repayment schedule, building up institutional capacity, and close monitoring and supervision.

(ii) *Institutional Development Programme*

This programme, initiated by ADBN in cooperation with GTZ, aims to increase outreach to women clients in various parts of Nepal. The strategy calls for the creation of farmers' institutions at the grassroots level which will also serve as financial intermediaries to their members. One women's cooperative has already been established and handed over to women to manage by themselves. The programme has already benefited 778 groups with 5,426 women members.[14]

(iii) *Linkage project between Government and banks*

The recently established Micro-Credit Project for Rural Women (MCPW) complements the Production Credit for Rural Women (PCRW) programme implemented by the Ministry of Local Development. PCRW has links with participating banks like ADBN, Rastriya Banijya Bank and Nepal Bank Ltd. To provide microcredit to women, two commercial banks have links to MCPW.

(iv) *Growth of regional rural development banks and NGOs*

The regional rural development banks (RRDB) are focusing their credit and savings services on poor Nepali women. These banks follow the basic philosophy and procedures of Grameen banking. A number of NGOs led by Nirdhan, which pattern their principles and practices from the Grameen Bank of Bangladesh, are also being established.

---

[14] Ishwari Shah, 1997. "Access of Women to Formal Credit and Financial Institutions in Nepal: Present Issues and Recent Developments in Policies and Practices". Paper presented at the Regional Seminar on Improving the Access of Women to Formal Credit in Least Developed Countries, Hanoi, Viet Nam, 1-4 July 1997.

(v) *Women farmers' revolving fund*

The creation of a Women Development Division in the Ministry of Agriculture has paved the way for the establishment of a women farmers' revolving fund as part of a special package programme that includes training, credit and technical support. The credit aspect is channelled through ADBN.

Despite recent developments in small farmer credit and microfinance activities, the issue of limited programme outreach remains. The sustainability of such programmes is also in question since most of them are costly to administer because of the high service delivery cost for many small loans.[15] Other pressing issues include the donor dependency of those microfinance programmes as well as programme coverage which duplicates microfinance services in certain geographic areas and by-passes others which need these services.

5. Innovative lessons from other countries

Practices for removing barriers to formal credit access have been developed in India, the Philippines, Thailand and Viet Nam as a result of enabling policy environment and institutional arrangements for microfinance.

The Reserve Bank of India has directed and encouraged all Indian commercial banks to link directly with NGOs and SHGs in order to reach the rural poor. Government and banking sector policy support has resulted in the widespread adoption of bank-NGO-SHG linkage schemes initially promoted by the National Bank for Agriculture and Rural Development. The linkage mechanism has substantially reduced transaction costs where banks have used NGOs and SHGs as the non-bank financial intermediaries.[16]

In Thailand, the Bank for Agriculture and Agricultural Cooperatives (BAAC) has recently been working directly with farmer groups, although earlier it had focused on individual borrowers. BAAC has also aggressively promoted savings mobilization schemes as a strategy for strengthening its microfinance activities. It has designed innovative savings products such as a savings deposit card, a farmer-housewife savings promotion scheme, a health care card scheme and a multiple fortune savings deposit. The latter promotes continuous savings through prizes that can be won in a series of lotteries. To attract more depositors among the poor, only a small (a minimum of 50 baht) initial savings deposit is required.

The Vietnam Bank for the Poor (VBP) and the Vietnam Bank for Agriculture and Rural Development provide small loans which do not need to be covered by physical collateral, mobile banking in remote areas, and cost-effective transaction offices operated only by a credit officer, a cashier and an accountant. Women farmers and micro-entrepreneurs are able to access government loans through VBP.

---

[15] Ibid.

[16] McGuire, P. B. and John D. Conroy. "Bank-NGO Linkages and the Transaction Costs of Lending to the Poor through Groups: Evidence from India and the Philippines", in Hartmut Schneider, ed., *Microfinance for the Poor?* (Development Centre Seminars, IFAD/OECD, 1997), p. 82.

NGOs in the Philippines, through aggressive advocacy on banking with the poor and the replication of the Grameen Bank principles and methodology, have assisted the government and the formal banking sector in meeting the increased demand for loans and savings facilities by women and the poor. Since 1990, the government has been launching microcredit programmes funded by several multilateral and bilateral agencies, including the Asian Development Bank (ADB) and the Canadian International Development Agency (CIDA).[17] The deregulation of banking has also resulted in the proliferation of bank and non-bank financial institutions.

Linkages were also started between banks and NGOs. Many microcredit NGOs were able to use commercial banks as sources of social funds, which were then on-lent to their clients at the market rate of interest. High loan recovery rates attested to the fact that access to credit was a more important limiting factor than high interest rates. The leading rural-based and government-owned commercial bank, Land Bank of the Philippines has indirectly recognized the market potential of banking with the poor. The Land Bank of the Philippines has spearheaded the creation of the People's Credit and Finance Corporation (PCFC) to service the credit requirement of the poor. PCFC has become the formal credit source for Grameen Bank replicators linked to NGOs and other lending to the poor.[18] Experiments have been widely undertaken on linking banks and self-help group projects funded by GTZ.

C. General observations and recommendations

General observations on policies and practices, and issues faced by countries are presented in this section. Together with these observations, a number of recommendations are made on further improving access by women to formal credit and financial institutions, especially in the least developed countries of the Asian and Pacific region.

1. Enabling policy environment

An enabling policy environment which promotes access of women to formal credit exists in those countries of South Asia and South-East Asia which have more developed formal financial systems. Countries in transition from centrally-planned to market-oriented economies should incorporate banking regulations to lower barriers to access by to formal credit as formal financial structures develop.

---

[17] The Asian Development Bank financed the microenterprises promoted by the Department of Trade and Industry (DTI) through credit and training, while the Canadian International Development Agency wholly funded another Grameen replication in Negros Occidental province of the Philippines. The province was then suffering from the collapse of the local sugar industry which was gravely affecting families of farm workers.

[18] *The Philippine Star*, Special Section, 8 August 1997, pp. S-13 and S-21.

It is recommended that regulations supportive of growth, development and expansion of microfinance institutions and non-bank financial intermediaries be formulated and implemented, since those institutions have the largest impact on increasing access by women to formal credit. To encourage savings deposits and improve the legality of NGO and microfinance institutions, it will be necessary to establish policies and regulations on mobilizing savings and formalizing accountability for funds entrusted to NGOs and microfinance institutions.

2. Outreach

In Bangladesh, India, Nepal, the Philippines and Viet Nam, where microfinance for women has already made convincing headway, the issue of outreach remains. While microfinance institutions or microfinance programmes of formal banks and government agencies have proven the success of micro-lending and savings principles and practices, those institutions still face constraints in expanding their operations. The difficulties have arisen as a result of insufficient funds to cover social preparation costs, initial overhead costs and additional capital necessary for repeat loans.

It is recommended that governments and donor agencies assist NGOs, microfinance institutions and microfinance programmes through financing social mobilization costs such as village visits, group formation, and the training of potential clients and staff. Seed money for on-lending and funds for repeat loans could be made accessible to intermediaries at cost. Formal banks should allocate a proportion of their loan portfolio to micro-lending. Government and donor agencies may provide guarantees to induce compliance by banks.

3. Linkage mechanisms

A majority of the countries in this study either have or are about to experiment with the concept and mechanics of linking banks with self-help groups through pilot projects. Micro-lending transaction costs of banks can be reduced if NGOs and SHGs are used as intermediaries to enable access to credit and savings services. However, accountability of such NGOs and SHGs are matters of concern to the banks as well as group members.

Given the success of the linkage model as an indirect method to disburse formal loans to clients, it is recommended that governments initiate and promote the implementation and development of linkage mechanisms which ensure the establish-ment of viable and sustainable intermediaries. An accreditation policy and method to determine the capabilities of NGOs and SHGs to act as intermediaries could be adopted.

4. Group technology

The concept of lending to individuals in a cohesive group, such as joint liability group (JLG), village solidarity group (VSG), or self-help group (SHG), is linked to cost-effective banking. Transaction costs in lending and borrowing can be reduced if banks and microfinance institutions deal directly with organized groups of borrowers rather than with many individual borrowers of small loans.

To be valuable collateral, the credit and saving discipline of the group must be maintained. It is therefore important to form groups through voluntary self-selection and common needs, rather than by an institutionally-enforced mechanism. Groups of poor and illiterate members require thorough training and social-technical preparation to handle the savings of their members, disburse loans and collect payments from members.

Recognizing that group collateral has become a common alternative to physical collateral, the legal definition of a group as a borrower needs to be addressed by policy makers. Such clarification will increase trust and confidence of the banks and intermediaries in those groups.

5. Credit tied to savings

Savings ensure sustainability and self-reliance. Previous credit programmes and institutions have failed because of the lack of savings mobilization and deposit-taking. To be sustainable, current microfinance institutions, microfinance programmes, NGOs and SHGs should emphasize the need to mobilize savings among group members.

It is recommended that in order to ensure sustainability of those institutions, savings mobilization among members and villagers should be of prime concern. It is also important to legally allow those institutions to collect savings from their members, even though they are not banks mandated by law.

When savings are mobilized from group members before loans are disbursed, credit discipline is enhanced. Every group member who contributed to the group fund will seek to ensure that their savings are wisely used and repaid by other group members. Promotion of internally-generated funds through savings, like the unit *desa* or village cooperative system in Indonesia, should be pursued aggressively.

6. Interest rates

Most successful microfinance institutions and microfinance programmes operate at market rates of interest, both for lending and saving. Formal banks regard loans exclusively for the poor as social credit rather than regular loans.

To be sustainable in their operations and in servicing debt capital, microfinance institutions have to charge market-oriented interest rates that account for inflation, default losses, administrative costs as well as opportunity costs of funds.

7. Subsidies

One of the major criticisms against microfinance institutions and NGOs is the high level of subsidy cost incurred in running the operations of such institutions. It has been admitted that banking with the poor is indeed difficult and expensive. Social mobilization work in remote areas, as well as training of illiterate clients and group officers, require considerable outlays in costs. This aspect of microfinance institutions and NGOs could be subsidized by government and donor agencies. Doorstep credit delivery, deposit collection and dedicated service by staff should match the market interest rates.

To counter the high initial costs faced by microfinance institutions in servicing the poor, it is recommended that donor and aid agencies, together with governments, should mobilize funds for the social preparation of clients before they receive loans, and for institutional and human resource development costs. Many microfinance institutions and microfinance programmes can then operate and expand, increasing access by women to financial institutions other than banks. Donor or government subsidies can be withdrawn as microfinance institutions develop the capacity for operational and financial self-sufficiency.

8. Revolving funds

In countries where banking facilities are absent or inaccessible, people in rural areas can access loans only through revolving funds. In the Lao People's Democratic Republic, for example, revolving funds were successful only during the first few cycles of operations due to non-repayments and defaults. Erosion of loan portfolios as a result of defaulting must therefore be prevented. Efficient loan recovery as well as aggressive savings deposit mobilization should result in a sustainable recycling of funds, in order to benefit a greater number of clients.

Policies and practices to enhance access by women to formal credit should create financial systems which efficiently deal with small transactions.[19] Through slow but sure steps, using simple and easy procedures, such policies and practices should make it possible for greater numbers of people to be regarded as credit-worthy and for those people to form long-term relationships with formal financial institutions.

---

[19] Adams, D. W. and J. D. Von Pischke, "Microenterprise Credit Programmes: Deja Vu", *World Development*, vol. 20, No. 10 (1992), pp. 1463-1470.

PART THREE

COUNTRY STUDY: VIET NAM[1]

A. Overview of involvement of women in economic activities and their financial requirements

1. Status of Vietnamese women

Poverty in Viet Nam has a heavy impact on women, especially those living in the rural areas. Although social statistics display an improvement in the overall position of women, inequalities between the sexes persist. The formal mass organization for women, the Vietnam Women's Union (VWU), which was established in 1930, has played a significant role in trying to improve the socio-economic life of women.

Table III.1. Status of women in Viet Nam

	Female	Male	Total
Population, 1994 (millions)	36 551	34 560	71 111
Life expectancy, 1994	72.6	68	
Illiteracy 1992 (percentage – 10 years and older)	17.7	8.6	
Mortality (percentage), 1989			
Infant	45.5	46.3	
Children (1 to 4 years)	6.6	5.4	
Maternal (per 100,000 live births, in 1993)	115-200		
Total fertility rate (birth per woman, in 1994)	3.1		
Education: gross enrolment ratios, as a percentage of school age population (1995)			
Primary	84	84.9	
Secondary	19.3	27.2	
Tertiary (female share of total) 1994	22.8		
Women at state management (percentage, 1992)	13.3		
Proportion of women among accused persons (percentage)	20.7		

Sources: Vietnam Women's Union and General Statistical Office; World Bank International Economics Department, April 1996; and Police Publishing House, *Crime in Viet Nam*, 1994.

---

[1] Prepared by Phan Ke Hoang, Director, Human Resource Development and Training, Vietnam Bank for Agriculture and Rural Development (VBARD), in collaboration with Nguyen Ngoc Tuyen, Vice-Director, VBARD Tuyen Quang, and Le Thanh Chung, Economist, Training Department, VBARD.

As shown in table III.1, the female population is larger than the male population; Vietnamese women comprise about 51 per cent of the total population. Infant and child mortality rates are almost the same for females and males. As a result of improved nutrition and birth control in Viet Nam in recent years, the maternal mortality rate has been reduced from 260 deaths per 100,000 live births in 1989 to 66 deaths per 100,000 live births in 1993 (according to UNDP). The fertility rate also declined from 4.6 births per woman in the mid-1980s to 3.1 births per woman in the early 1990s.

Disparities, however, are apparent in education. There are twice as many illiterate women than men in Viet Nam. Although the rates for primary school enrolment are the same for both sexes, the enrolment rate for women who attend secondary school is less than half of that for men. Furthermore, women comprise only 23 per cent of students in higher education.

Box III.1. Vietnamese economy in brief

Viet Nam, located in South-East Asia, covers 331,033 square kilometres and has an estimated population of 71 million. The rural Vietnamese economy is mainly agrarian and relies on rice production for both domestic consumption and exports. In 1993, farming occupied 65 per cent of the workforce, generated 40 per cent of the gross national product (GNP) and accounted for 50 per cent of exports. (*Labour Review*, 14 September 1996) In 1993, Viet Nam became the third largest rice exporter after Thailand and the United States, with an exported rice volume of 2 million tons. (Le Van Toan, *Viet Nam Socio-economy 1991/1992*)

Poverty reduction has been a central goal of the government since reunification and a driving force behind a series of economic reforms initiated in 1989. The annual growth rate of gross domestic product (GDP) during the 1990s is estimated at 8 per cent. But despite recent economic growth, Viet Nam remains a low-income country with a per capita GDP of less than US$ 200. According to the Ministry of Labour, Invalids and Social Affairs, 20 per cent of the total population live below the poverty line and 90 per cent of the poor live in rural areas.

The country has been aggressively implementing conservative monetary and fiscal policies. As a result, the inflation rate of 4.5 per cent recorded in 1996 was much lower than the 100 per cent annual inflation rate recorded in the mid-1980s (Population Census and General Statistics Office). Viet Nam has succeeded in controlling the government deficit and that stability has given foreign investors more confidence in investing in Viet Nam. As of 30 June 1993, 588 projects were proceeding, represent-ing a cumulative capital of US$ 6.2 billion, of which US$ 1.5 billion has actually been invested.

In 1996 Viet Nam become the seventh member of the Association of South East Asian Nations (ASEAN).

---

2. Overview of involvement of women in economic activities

The participation of women in the economy has increased considerably since reunification in 1975 and the implementation of economic reforms, beginning in 1986 (table III.2). There are significant differences in the sources of income according to region. Of the seven economic regions in the country, this study focuses on the two main regions: the north around the Red River Delta and the south around the Mekong River Delta. Because of smaller sizes of land holdings in the north, the poor female-led households work on the farm, while wealthier households have incomes from non-farm sources. The situation is reversed in the south, where poor female-led households rely heavily on income from non-farm sources and well-off households concentrate on farm activities. Women are traditionally considered as the "safe-box keepers" who control family finances and are therefore the first to borrow during famines or other periods of economic difficulty.

Table III.2. Workforce

(Unit: '000)

Age group	1979			1989			1994		
	Total	Women	Men	Total	Women	Men	Total	Women	Men
16-54	23 645	12 493	11 152	31 210	16 411	14 799	35 102	18 363	16 739
16-59	25 198	13 365	11 833	33 155	17 458	15 697	37 165	19 555	17 610
15-59	26 571	14 030	12 541	34 569	18 150	16 419	38 733	20 337	18 396

Source: General Statistics Office, *Population Census 1979, 1989.* General Statistics Office, *Inter-censal Demographic Survey 1994.*

A General Statistics Office (GSO) survey conducted in 1989, both in urban and rural areas noted that the number of the women in the workforce was greater than that of men. Using the International Labour Organization (ILO) definition, the gap between men and women in the workforce has become even greater. The annual growth rate of women in the workforce is quite high, standing at 2.87 per cent during 1979-1989 and 2.25 per cent in 1989-1994 (table III.2). It is still lower than the growth rate of men in the workforce. According to the 1994 census, female economic activity rates rose in both rural and urban areas, but the increase was more rapid in urban areas as a result of the urbanization and industrialization that began in the late 1980s.

In the newly formed market economy of Viet Nam, both males and females participate in the workforce as soon as possible. This may explain the decline in secondary and tertiary enrolment for the period 1987-1993.[2] Women in both rural and

---

[2] *Educational Year Book 1994,* Ministry of Education and Training, General Statistics Office.

29

urban areas start to work about one year earlier than men. According to the 1992/1993 Vietnamese Living Standard Survey, rural women start working one and a half years earlier than their urban counterparts (rural household income is about half that of urban households). The number of women aged 13-14 and 15-19 involved in economic activity is higher than their male counterparts. In other age groups the situation is reversed (table III.3). The female unemployment rate in all age groups is less than the male unemployment rate.

According to the 1994 survey by the World Bank, 71 per cent of the workforce was engaged in the agricultural sector and 14 per cent was involved in the industrial sector. Women in rural areas are largely involved in agricultural and food processing activities such as the production of rice, potatoes, sweet potato, cassava and groundnuts in the north, and coffee, cashew and grapes in the south. Post-harvest work includes food drying, milling and dehusking. Livestock raising by women includes pigs, cattle and goats in mountainous areas, and cattle together with fowl, ducks and chickens in the delta region. Growth in the domestic and export markets is providing employment for women in raising turtles, crocodiles, snakes and prawns.

Women assist in land preparation, tilling, timber cutting and fishing. Women from rural areas are engaged in small trading of agricultural products such as rice, corn, fruit and meats to earn extra income during the peak season. Women also migrate to cities and work as cooks, waitresses or household help. Some women also operate shops, carry out tailoring and undertake inter-provincial trading either from north to south or with China. The number of women family labourers who are not recorded in official statistics is undoubtedly high.

Table III.3. Gender distribution of the workforce and unemployment (rate by age group, 1989)

(Unit: percentage)

Age group	Economic activity rate		Unemployment rate	
	Women	Men	Women	Men
Total	71.3	77.5	5.4	6.2
13-14	38.0	30.1	25.9	29.2
15-19	73.5	67.7	16.3	17.8
20-24	88.8	94.4	6.6	8.3
25-29	89.3	97.4	2.7	3.9
30-34	88.1	97.3	1.4	2.5
35-39	86.9	95.7	0.9	1.5
40-44	83.9	91.8	0.6	1.2
45-49	78.7	86.9	0.3	1.0
50-54	69.4	81.2	0.3	0.7
55-59	54.2	70.9	0.2	0.5
60-64	35.6	53.1	0.1	0.3
65+	13.2	27.2	0.2	0.1

Source: General Statistics Office, *Population Census 1989*, detailed analysis of sample results 1991.

Compared to men, women have less choice. It has been reported that because in Vietnamese society highly educated women are not considered desirable as wives, the education of boys is preferred. Table III.1 indicates that the highest level of education most girls achieve is secondary school. In large poor rural families, girls must end school quickly and pave the way for their brothers.

Table III.4 details the gap between male and female distribution in vocational and higher education. The number of girls attending professional school, the graduates of which are considered to be semi-skilled workers, was slightly higher than their male counterparts in the late 1980s, but significantly less in the early 1990s.

Table III.4. Number of students in vocational, college and university, 1985-1994

(Unit: '000 persons)

	1985-1986		1986-1987		1993-1994	
	Men	Women	Men	Women	Men	Women
Vocational	59.1	69.4	68.2	70.6	59.9	21.2
Tertiary	53.0	35.6	52.6	35.2	84.4	34.2
	(Unit: percentage)					
Sex structure:						
Vocational	46.0	54.0	48.1	51.9	73.9	26.1
Tertiary	59.8	40.2	61.4	38.6	71.2	28.8

Sources: *Statistical Year Book 1986,* General Statistics Office; and *Educational Statistics Yearbook 1994,* Education and Training Ministry.

After leaving secondary school, women join vocational centres, normally for two years, to receive training in tailoring, construction, health care, bookkeeping, and audio-video repair. They work for lower wages than those who have completed high school after four to five years of study. According to Ministry of Education and Training, the proportion of female students is lower than male students in all academic fields, with the exception of teacher training.

Because the centrally-planned economy controlled all sectors until 1986, university students joined State-owned enterprises (SOEs) or government offices after graduation. Although the State does not officially distinguish between men and women when selecting its recruits, men are preferred in terms of postings and transfers. Since implementation of the "open door" policy and the new law encouraging foreign investment in late 1980, foreign companies have recruited highly educated staff and paid them five to 10 times more than the State sector. This brain drain is occurring throughout the country and is not limited to qualified women. Many, especially those who are fluent in foreign languages, move from SOEs to foreign firms to work as office staff or secretaries. In SOEs, welfare is better and more free time is available but few women are able to become SOEs leaders. Many women are also engaged in private business with support from their husbands.

The distribution of women in the different sectors is presented in table III.5. The female workforce is centred mainly in the public economic sector. In this category, women outnumber men by 10 per cent. The private sector is still underdeveloped but employment should increase quickly as highly educated staff move from the State sector to other areas.

Table III.5. Gender distribution of employment by type of enterprise, 1994

(Unit: percentage)

	Women	Men
Household economic sector (public)	76.4	67.8
Private enterprise sector	10.3	16.4
Cooperatives	0.7	1.7
Joint venture	0.6	0.9
Government	12.1	13.1

Source: Ministry of Labour, *11 Eastern South Provinces Survey*, 1994.

Whether working for the public, private or State sector, monthly wages of men are usually higher than those paid to women by 30 per cent at the national level (table III.6). According to Ministry of Labour, Invalids and Social Affairs, women in SOEs now stop working four years earlier than they did in the 1980s. In urban areas, men are better remunerated than women at all education levels. In rural areas, well-educated women receive higher pay than men. Female university graduates are scarce in rural areas and most would like to be employed in cities after graduation.

Table III.6. Average monthly wage by areas and qualification, 1992-1993

(Unit: thousand dong)

Level of education	Urban		Rural	
	Women	Men	Women	Men
No diploma	142	218	61	101
Primary	172	273	66	94
Secondary	176	265	105	92
Vocational	163	270	105	157
Tertiary	247	343	137	131

Source: *Viet Nam Living Standards Survey 1992-1993*, General Statistics Office and State Planning Committee, 1994.

Table III.7 indicates the gender distribution of sectoral employment. More women than men participate in the agricultural sector, and women outnumber men by almost 2.5 times in the trading and service sectors.

Table III.7. Gender distribution of sectoral employment, 1989

Sector	Total ('000)	Sex structure (percentage)		Sectoral structure (percentage)		
		Women	Men	Total	Women	Men
Total	28 791	52	48	100.0	100.0	100.0
1. Industrial	3 014	43	57	10.5	8.6	12.5
2. Construction	540	27	73	1.9	1.0	2.8
3. Agriculture and forestry	21 355	53	47	74.1	76.0	72.2
4. Transport and communication	504	17	83	1.7	0.5	3.0
5. Trading and services	1 800	69	31	6.2	8.3	4.1
6. Other	1 578	53	47	5.5	5.6	5.4

Source: *Population Census 1989*, General Statistics Office.

2. Financial requirements of women

In urban areas women need financing for trading, shopkeeping, or operating small businesses. In rural areas, women typically need small amounts of credit for their micro businesses related to agro-processing. Women farmers also need financing for agricultural inputs including seeds, fertilizers, pesticides, insecticides or even food to carry them through until harvest.

According to World Bank estimates, the formal financial sector in Viet Nam has the capacity to serve only 25 per cent of the population. Women find it difficult to borrow, and even when an application is approved, the loan is often not extended as desired. The ADB team project 1961 VIE, which surveyed women borrowers in Tuyen Quang province in 1994, found that women received only 50 per cent of the required loans and faced a far shorter repayment period.

Poor women who are less educated and have no land title deed find it difficult to gain access to formal credit and consequently turn to the informal sector. The situation is more serious when women seek urgent financial assistance in times of disasters or food shortage, or when they need medical help. Poor women have access to informal lenders, who extend loans for various purposes, but charge high interest rates and place strict conditions on repayment. To overcome such restrictions, schemes by VBP and various NGOs have been established to grant loans to the poor. The informal sector still exists and soft loans are not available for poor women. Recommendations on how to strengthen formal financial institutions will be discussed in later sections of this study.

B. Overview of existing formal, semi-formal and informal financial facilities

The financial sector in Viet Nam can be separated into the formal, semi-formal and informal sectors. The formal sector consists of financial institutions governed by the Law on Banks and Financial Institutions and regulated by the State Bank of Viet Nam. Local and international donor agencies and NGOs that provide credit are considered semi-formal facilities and are a sub-module of the formal sector. The informal sector consists of individual or group lenders who are not regulated by State Bank of Viet Nam regulations. The informal sector has been the dominant lending facility. A recent UNDP/Swedish International Development Agency (SIDA)-financed Vietnam Living Standard Survey, which sampled 4,800 households, indicated that the informal sector provided 70 per cent of all loans and the formal sector provided the remaining 30 per cent.

1. Formal financial sector

The formal financial sector was established in the late 1980s when the State Bank of Viet Nam dismantled its monopoly and switched to a two-tiered system comprising itself and the commercial banking system. By the end of 1994, Viet Nam's financial system comprised the State Bank of Viet Nam, four State-owned commercial banks, 46 shareholding banks, three joint-venture banks, 13 foreign bank branches, 69 credit cooperatives, 153 People's Credit Funds, two finance companies and one insurance company (table III.8). In August 1995, the Government of Viet Nam established the specialized Vietnam Bank for the Poor to strengthen credit support it proved to the poor.

Total banking assets were about dong 38.8 trillion in 1993, which was only about 30 per cent of GDP. This figure is low in comparison with other countries in Asia and indicates that Viet Nam is under-utilizing its financial capacity. Banks are estimated to serve less than 25 per cent of the population in Viet Nam. Banks have nevertheless adopted many changes since the implementation of financial reforms in the early 1990s. The proportion of credit given by the banking system to the private sector, particularly in agriculture and trade, has been increasing. The Vietnam Bank for Agriculture and Rural Development (VBARD), for example, has increased its lending portfolio to households and expanded its financing facilities through joint liability groups. (The key role of VBARD in rural finance will be explained in the subsection below on rural financial institutions.) Despite that expansion, the demand for credit far outstrips the capacity of the financial system.

(a) *State-owned commercial banks*

The banking sector is dominated by the four State-owned commercial banks. In 1994 they accounted for about 90 per cent of all assets in the banking system. That figure had declined to less than 80 per cent by early 1997, as a result of the expanding operations of foreign banks. The four State-owned commercial banks are:

Table III.8. Structure of the financial system as of December 1994

Institution	Assets (in trillion dong)	Number	Number of branches	Capital and reserves
State Bank of Viet Nam	43.7		53 provincial	D 500 billion
Commercial Banks	48.4			Minimum capital of each bank: US$ 20 million (D 20 billion)
1. State-owned banks	43.3			D 2 114 billion Actual capital and reserves
Bank for Foreign Trade of Vietnam	16.1		14 provincial	D 485 billion
Viet Nam Bank for Agriculture and Rural Development	9.6		56 provincial, 500 district	D 597 billion
Bank for Investment and Development of Viet Nam	7.6		53 provincial, 41 district	D 658 billion
Industrial and Commercial Bank	10.1		50 provincial, 37 district	D 374 billion
2. Other reporting banks	5.1			D 673 billion
(a) Joint-stock banks				Minimum capital
Urban		30		D 20 billion; D 50 billion for banks in Hanoi; D 70 billion for banks in Ho Chi Minh City
Rural		16		D 1 billion (without branches) D 3 billion (with branches)
(b) Joint venture banks		3		US$ 10 million
(c) Foreign bank branches (licensed)		13		US$ 15 million (nine banks operating)
Others				
3. Credit cooperatives		69		D 300 million
4. People's Credit Funds (licensed)		153		
5. Finance companies		2		D 10 billion
6. Insurance companies		1		

Source: Financial Investment Department, State Bank of Viet Nam.

(i) *Industrial and Commercial Bank of Vietnam (INCOMBANK)*

INCOMBANK was created from the industrial and commercial loan department of SBV, and took over the SBV urban branch network, comprising 35 provincial and 60 district offices. Of its total loan portfolio of D 113 trillion in 1989, 33 per cent was in industrial loans, 31 per cent in commercial loans and 19 per cent in agricultural loans.

(ii) *Vietnam Bank for Agriculture and Rural Development (VBARD)*

VBARD, which was created from the Agricultural Credit Department of SBV, took over the SBV rural branch network. Of its total loan portfolio at that time, only 40 per cent comprised agricultural production loans. The balance consisted of loans in trading related to agricultural inputs and products. At present, VBARD plays a critical role in rural lending in Viet Nam. Details of this bank will be discussed in a later section.

(iii) *Bank for Foreign Trade of Vietnam (VIETCOMBANK)*

This bank, established in 1963 with a monopoly in export and import finance, has branches in 10 cities. With the financial reforms, it has lost its monopoly and is now highly subsidized by the State.

(iv) *Bank for Investment and Development of Vietnam (BIDV)*

BIDV was designated as a development bank to finance infrastructure and social sector projects, as well as commercial projects. The bank is not allowed to accept deposits with maturities of less than one year. Since a large proportion of domestic savings is short-term, savings mobilization capacity of BIDV is minimal.

Table III.9 shows the deposits and loans of the four types of banks detailed above, as of December 1996. The State-owned commercial banks share 73 per cent of total deposits and 75 per cent of total loans. Joint stock banks ranked second place with 14 per cent of deposits and 12 per cent of loans. These two type of domestic commercial banks thus dominate the financial market in Viet Nam.

Table III.9. Deposits and loans by type of bank, 1996

(Data compiled from 28 banks)

Type of bank	Deposits		Loans	
	Value (billion D)	Percentage share of total	Value (in billion D)	Percentage share of total
State-owned commercial banks	30 538	73.6	38 320	75.0
Joint-stock banks	5 887	14.3	5 701	11.8
Foreign banks	2 842	6.8	5 375	10.6
Joint venture banks	2 185	5.3	1 355	2.6

Source: Economics Research Department, State Bank of Viet Nam, 1996.

As shown in table III.10, 53 per cent of the total credit was extended to the public sector, while 47 per cent was given to the private sector (agriculture and trade, which involve a high participation rate of women). Since 90 per cent of the loans were granted to State-owned enterprises until the late 1980s, this marks a significant change in bank loan composition.

Table III.10. Sectoral distribution of commercial bank loans, 1996

Sector	Share of total loans (percentage)
1. **Public sector**	**52.8**
Industry	29.6
Construction	14.5
Transport and communication	2.6
Other	6.1
2. **Private sector**	**47.2**
Agriculture	20.4
Trade	26.8

Source: Economic Research Department, State Bank of Viet Nam, 1996.

(b) *Non-public financial institutions*

In addition to the four State-owned commercial banks, a number of non-public financial institutions are providing loans to women: (a) rural credit cooperatives; (b) shareholding banks or commercial joint stock banks; and (c) foreign banks and joint venture banks. The rural credit cooperatives and shareholding banks operate mainly in the countryside. Foreign banks emerged after financial liberalization which ended the monopoly held by the Bank for Foreign Trade of Viet Nam. The number of foreign banks and joint venture banks remains small at present, but is likely to increase within the decade.

(c) *Non-bank financial institutions*

Non-bank financial institutions were recognized under the 1990 banking law. Today, there are only two non-bank financial companies operating in Viet Nam: the Saigon Joint Stock Finance Company and Seaprodex Finance Company. These two finance companies are in the experimental stage and are reported to be unable to meet international standards.

2. Semi-formal financial sector

(a) *Donor agencies*

Two types of donor agencies provide semi-formal finance in Viet Nam:

(a)   Bilateral programmes with other governments (Australian, Czech, Danish, French, German and Swedish) provide funds primarily for job creation for return migrants in the fields like agro-processing, irrigation and forestry. Credit of this type is limited and the Government of Viet Nam undertakes responsibility as a direct debtor;

(b) Multilateral programmes with ADB, the World Bank, IFAD, the United Nations Population Fund (UNFPA), the United Nations Children's Fund (UNICEF), the World Food Programme, the Food and Agriculture Organization of the United Nations (FAO), the European Union and the International Rice Research Institute provide assistance in agriculture, irrigation, environmental protection, natural resource management and technical assistance. A large proportion of the funds have been extended as grants.

Funds are channelled to the poor and women through banks, local people's authorities, academic institutions like the Vietnam Institute for Agriculture Science and Technology, government agencies such as the Department of Agriculture and Rural Development (DARD), or directly to borrowers through joint liability groups, as in the case of the Viet Nam-Sweden Forestry Cooperation Programme.

(b) *International non-governmental organizations*

Of the 250 foreign NGOs in Viet Nam, at least 17, including Oxfam, Save the Children's Fund and Catholic Relief Credit, are reported to be extending credit to the rural poor. The credit and savings modules of NGOs are largely designed for joint liability groups, and are granted either in collaboration with banks such as the VBARD or with local government offices, local NGOs or mass organizations such as the Vietnamese Women's Union, Veterans Association, Youth Association or the Farmers Association.

A UNDP survey in 1996 reviewed selected saving and credit schemes sponsored by foreign NGOs and assessed their interest rates. According to the survey findings, cooperation projects have focused on income improvement of rural households, rural development, safe water and birth control. The scale of the NGO programmes is small, averaging 1,265 people borrowing from loan funds of US$ 42,000 each, and entailing high operational costs. The results of the UNDP survey have confirmed that through NGO programmes in Viet Nam, poor women are able to undertake and repay loans at interest rates which are even higher than those offered by the main formal rural financial institutions.

3. Informal financial sector

The informal financial sector consists of entities that perform financial intermediation functions but are not subject to regulatory supervision by the State Bank of Viet Nam. They raise deposits for on-lending through their own funds, external aid funds or specific government funds. These informal lenders include *Roscas* or *tontines*, trader lenders, miller and farmer lenders as well as professional moneylenders, and can be grouped as detailed below.

The majority of credit provided by the informal sector has been from relatives at low interest rates, or from moneylenders at interest rates which are reasonable given the costs and risks involved. For small loans, the real cost of borrowing may be even lower than that of VBA. The 1994 Living Standard and Monetary Survey found that average money-lending rates to rural farmers were only 1 per cent higher than that of private banks, although such rates were double the rate charged by relatives or State-owned commercial banks. Having the advantages of flexibility and lack of collateral requirement, informal funds often accompanied VBA loans extended to farmers.

The informal sector still exists since the formal sector is unable to provide comprehensive service and choices to rural borrowers. Lengthy approval procedures, limited loan purposes and collateral requirements prevent rural women from borrowing from banks and force them to turn to moneylenders.

To get a deeper understanding of formal credit and financial institutions, it is important to look at their policies, procedures and practices of lending to the poor, and especially to poor women. Due to the lack of gender-disaggregated data in banks, assessing the credit status of women is difficult. The number of women borrowers in joint liability groups are recorded only by VBA and VBP. The figures for female individuals and household clients are estimates drawn from field visits and interviews with bank officers.

(a) *Friends and relatives*

Friends and relatives are major sources of loans which carry low or no interest. Loans in Vietnamese dong are short term, while loans in gold or US dollars are longer term.

(b) *Tontines (Roscas)*

Tontines (Roscas), also called *phuong, hui* or *ho*, have existed in Viet Nam for generations and have greatly increased in number, but have never been officially recognized. The *tontine* can be grouped as either the credit type or the supportive type. The credit *tontine* exists mainly for lending purposes, with the participants earning additional income from the interest earned. The supportive type of *tontine*, on the other hand, is a fund-raising scheme whose main goal is to pool funds for mutual assistance of its members rather than for earning interest. The latter existed before the credit type, and has been more widespread in Viet Nam. Supporting *tontines* can be interest-earning or non-interest-earning. As the experience in 1989-1990 showed, *tontines* have significant disadvantages: lack of legal security; high risk; and high possibility of default.

(c) *Private moneylenders*

Private moneylenders provided one-third of loans to Vietnamese households, according to the Vietnamese Living Standard Survey of 1994. The average interest rates charged by these lenders were higher than banks or other informal sources of loans. The average rate charged by private moneylenders was estimated at an annual 102 per cent. Those rates were three to five times greater than the interest rates charged by VBA and the cooperatives (the VBA average interest rate for household lending in 1994 was 39 per cent and the rate for cooperatives was 23 per cent). The terms of loan repayment are flexible, and can be in cash or in kind.

4. Formal rural financial institutions

This study concentrates on poor women, especially those living in rural areas, and examines their access to formal credit. Emphasis will therefore be placed on the policies, practices and procedures of rural financial units.

The formal financial institutions in Viet Nam located primarily in the rural areas include VBARD, VBP, credit cooperative, rural shareholding banks and People's Credit Funds. This study will address in detail the first two banks, which are the largest formal lenders to rural women.

(a) *Vietnam Bank for Agriculture and Rural Development*

Vietnam Bank for Agriculture and Rural Development (VBARD), known as Vietnam Bank for Agriculture prior to 1995, was founded in 1988, after the dismantling of the centrally-planned economy, to meet the increasing demand for credit among people in rural areas. VBARD is currently the largest formal lender and accounts for more than 90 per cent of formal sector loans in the countryside. It is the largest State-owned commercial bank in Viet Nam, with a staff of 20,000 and a system network divided into four levels: the headquarters in Hanoi, one regional representative office each in the Southern Region and the Central Region, 61 provincial branches and 4,500 district branches nationwide.

Although VBARD is permitted to undertake all banking functions, it has a rural credit mandate. VBARD switched from lending to State-owned enterprises, which accounted for 98 per cent of all loans, to lending to households which now account for 75 per cent of loans. As of December 1995, VBA loans had been made to more than 12 million rural households through various programmes, as shown in table III.11.

The average VBARD loan size is dong 1.3 million (US$ 113). Although most of the loans are extended directly to clients, some are indirectly disbursed through mass organizations with priority given to VWU. Because of the small loan sizes, large network and absence of incentive scheme for VBARD staff, transaction costs are high. The current interest rate spread is only 0.35 per cent per month, which is inadequate for the long-term sustainability of VBARD. The bank is therefore trying to balance its official and commercial functions.

A range of strategies has been implemented to ensure operational effectiveness in the commercial role of the bank. In order to be able to rely on its own sources rather than having to borrow from others, VBARD is aggressive in mobilizing funds. To create competition not only with other local commercial banks, but also among VBARD branches throughout Viet Nam, a financial contract is being applied throughout the VBARD system. The financial contract offers higher compensation to branches showing higher profits, in an attempt to force all branches to be more self-decisive and dynamic.

Table III.11. Vietnam Bank for Agriculture and Rural Development loans to households and the poor sector by lending programme (as of 30 May 1995)

(Unit: million dong)

Name of programme/project	Loan funds	Monthly interest rate		Purpose of project	Loans granted	Loans collected	Loans out-standing	Number of house-holds	Number of groups	Note
		Short term	Medium term							
1. World Bank project	636 338	2.1	1.7	Agriculture	861 152	265 171	595 981	267 872		Amount received 4 588
2. IFAD project	40 000	1.8; 2.1	1.7	Income generation	1 497	63	1 434	1 169		
3. EC programmes	198 309			Life stabilization micro-enterprises	339 216	129 327	209 880	21 981		Data as of 30 Nov. 1994
4. VBARD Project	5 000		2.1	Poverty alleviation	5 549	0	5 549	6 274	105	Lending interest rate of VBA: 2.1 per cent per month
5. Family planning project	1 000	1.8		Family planning	1 000	2	998	2 013	100	Awaiting extension
6. VIE 91/POI project	5 504	2.1			2 302	1 569	733	994	27	
7. Government poverty alleviation programme	428 600	1.2	1.2	Agricultural production	204 012	50	203 962	221 099	21 141	
8. Government of Germany-financed poverty alleviation project	55 138	1.2		Production	11 950		11 950	11 370	462	Amount received 15 600 until 8 August 1995
9. Credit programme				Agricultural/forestry development	26 804 489	19 856 765	7 343 724	11 910 175		
Total	1 369 889				28 231 167	19 856 947	8 374 211	12 442 945	21 835	

Source: Vietnam Bank for Agriculture and Rural Development.

Notes: Funds from foreign donors to VBARD total D 930,885.8 million.

Total EC funds disbursed: US$ 18,015,065, equivalent to D 198,309 million at an exchange rate D 11,008 to US$ 1.

Funds disbursed through IFAD projects total D 40,000 million.

Project T64: D 5,000 million of VBARD funds.

Family planning project: D 1,000 million, of which D 550.4 million is in project funds.

Project VIE 91/POI: US$ 50,000, equivalent to D 5,504 million at an exchange rate of D 11,008 to US$1.

Government of Germany poverty alleviation project: DM 7 million, equivalent to D 55,138.4 million, at an exchange rate of D 7,876.92 to DM 1.

VBARD is reaching potential customers in an effort to be a universal bank. With the principle that "the client is the boss", the bank provides package credit to enterprises to maximize interest income. A proportion of those profits will be retained to cover possible losses in lending to the poor. An example of a successful VBARD branch is illustrated in box III.2.

Box III.2. Son Duong Bank for Agriculture and Rural Development

Son Duong, located 160 kms north-west of Hanoi, is a mountainous district in Tuyen Quang province. The town of Son Duong town is located 35 kilometres from the town of Tuyen Quang and 75 kilometres from the furthest commune in the district.

The organizational chart of the 44 bank staff at VBARD Son Duong is shown below.

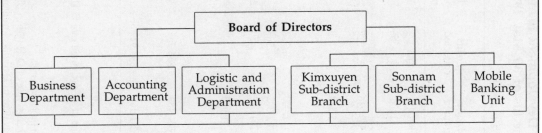

The Son Duong Bank for Agriculture and Rural Development has mobilized funds totalling D 42,631 million as of April 1997. Total loans outstanding are dong 38,361 million, of which 85 per cent are short term. The mandates and goals are to improve the life of people in the district through credit and savings, and to ensure sustainability.

As mentioned above, Son Duong bank operates in a remote area. A large proportion of loans are given in the isolated communes which can be reached only by motorbikes or push bikes. Loans are disbursed in small amounts (averaging dong 1,340,000) but often are not collected on time, thus leading to high operational costs.

Son Duong bank extends loans for forestry, agro-processing and small trade. Borrowers need financing to buy seedlings, animals, insecticide and production tools. In the past, Son Duong bank has had to cope with number of difficulties, including a lack of capital, a low level of funds mobilization, a lack of support facilities such as vehicles and computers, and an absence of a credit culture because of the underdevelopment of the market economy in the district.

Nevertheless, the bank has adopted many changes and has become a successful financial institution. The bank has been a catalyst in the improvement of the quality of life and economic growth in the district. In 1996, the number of poor households declined by 3.5 per cent. Economic growth of the district was estimated at 7.5 per cent per year in 1996. Son Duong bank also pays much attention to gender issues in lending. Women clients accounted for 45 per cent of total borrowers in 1996 and received loans through 193 joint liability groups, comprising of 1,998 poor households.

(Continued on next page)

The social welfare functions undertaken by VBARD lasted until the formation of the Vietnam Bank for the Poor (VBP) in August 1995. The social welfare role is now left to the VBP, and VBARD is operating purely as a commercial rural bank. VBARD extends concessionary funds only when required by the government for specific programmes. VBARD still acts as an agent for VBP in credit flow and is paid 3.5 per cent in total interest to cover operational costs. VBARD pays 10 per cent interest to its financial intermediaries such as joint liability groups.

Lending to the poor is costly because of the small size of the average loans as well as the fragmentation of rural finance. To attain social welfare goals, VBP extends loans to the poor through mass organizations and joint liability groups which act as the bank's agents to reduce transaction costs and to ensure collection of payments. To ensure continued preferential credit for the poor, VBARD and VBP need to strengthen human resources development through technical training. Furthermore, government support is vital to ensure the long-term sustainability of VBP, since it is now facing several problems, including a shortage of funds.

Demand for VBARD loans is great because the interest rate is correspondingly low at a monthly 1.25 per cent in the third quarter of 1996, compared with average monthly money-lending rates of 2 to 2.5 per cent. VBARD funds are therefore rationed, and tend to go to more wealthy applicants rather than to poor farmers. Poor women therefore seem to be neglected in the commercial lending activities of VBARD.

(b) *Vietnam Bank for the Poor*

VBP was officially established by Decision No. 252/TTG issued by the Prime Minister's Office, dated August 1995. The mission statement of VBP seeks to eliminate hunger and to reduce poverty based on the non-profit principle through the provision of credit and improvements in credit systems. VBP has its headquarters in Hanoi; a regional office will be set up in the south, using part of the VBARD network under an inter-agency agreement. In 1996, VBP aimed to extend loans to 1.5 million poor households and to reduce the current poor households ratio of 16 per cent down to 10 per cent by the year 2000.

VBP has had to cope with new challenges as a result of the monthly-lending rate of 1 per cent imposed by the government in the third quarter of 1996, while the deposit rate of commercial banks has remained at 0.9 per cent monthly. Furthermore, VBP loans are mortgage-free for over three years and can be used only for the purposes of production and trade. This has resulted in difficulty in mobilizing funds as well as the depletion of dong 1,400 billion in funds. The default rate, as officially reported, is over 3 per cent; however, this may actually be higher and losses have been incurred. Since the bank cannot simultaneously undertake the social welfare function and maintain financial sustainability, it needs to be restructured.

(i) *Structure and policies*

State rural sector microfinancing, including lending to women, suffers from distortions arising from macroeconomic policies. VBARD and the VBP are expected to become sustainable (i.e., self-funding) institutions, but they are also mandated social welfare objectives. They lend at lower interest rates than that offered by urban banks. Attention to transaction costs is not as rigorous as it should be. Real costs of borrowing, especially for small loans, may not be lower than commercial lending.

(ii) *Lending rates*

The current VBARD and VBP lending rates are positive in real terms but the spread is too thin to cover operational costs. At 1.25 per cent per month in the third quarter of 1996, lending rates set by VBARD and VBP are about half of money-lending rates. Demand for VBARD and VBP loans is therefore extremely high. For many not-so-poor women, funds are not available on a regular basis. Furthermore, the key formal rural institutions in Viet Nam are only capable of financing the relatively wealthier and very poor women, and the majority of women depend on the informal sector.

At the APRACA-VBARD-GTZ consultation workshop on microfinance, held in Hanoi in October 1996, it was recommended that formal lenders raise their lending rates to market rates. However, since all formal rural sector lending in Viet Nam is at low fixed-interest rates, the determination of market rates is difficult. In addition, the rural market is highly segmented as a result of the difficult geographic terrain and a lack of information. Usurious rates may prevail because of the absence of available credit or competition. Even when a range of options is available, some women may still select local moneylenders at higher interest rates than VBARD after accounting for all real costs of borrowing.

(c) *Credit cooperatives*

Credit cooperatives came into being in Viet Nam around 1956 in the north, and in 1983 in the south. At its peak the number of credit cooperatives nationwide numbered 7,180; however, most of those cooperatives have collapsed, and at present there are no more than 160, operating mainly in urban areas, near major highways or near aquaculture sites. Of those 160, only 32 are operating efficiently. The total liabilities of the cooperatives stood at dong 125.6 billion (US$ 18 million) by the end of 1990.

(d) *Rural shareholding banks*

Rural shareholding banks have recently emerged to replace credit cooperatives, but they have had minimal impact on lending and savings mobilization in rural Viet Nam. These generally small banks, with an average of 50 to 60 shareholders, are important source of funds in the south. Forty-four were licensed by 1995. The main weakness of rural shareholding banks is their reliance on VBARD as a source of funding. Between 50 and 80 per cent of their funds are borrowed from VBARD at a monthly interest rate of 2.6 per cent, and the funds are on-lent to farm households at a monthly interest rate of 3 per cent.

(e) *People's Credit Funds*

People's Credit Funds or People's Funds were introduced by the State Bank of Viet Nam in 1993 in 14 provinces (73 districts and 173 communes) because VBARD was not able to fill the vacuum left by the collapse of the rural credit cooperative system. Following the model of Quebec's Caisse Populaire system, the system is split into three levels (figure III.1).

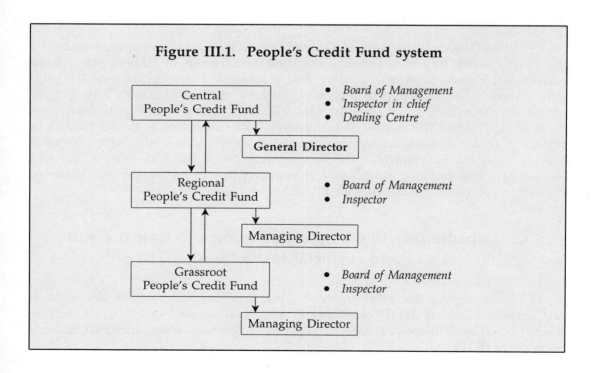

Figure III.1. People's Credit Fund system

The three levels are independent in their accounting, determination of profit and loss, and their assets control. The units are interlinked by shares at each level. In the case of a liquidity problem, the People's Credit Fund reconciles funds within its network to overcome its crisis.

In 1994, 40 per cent of the funding for the central fund came from the State Bank of Viet Nam, with the remainder being received from local and regional units through members' shares and deposits. The purchase of shares is a precondition for loan approval. Loans are provided primarily for agricultural uses, including crop production and livestock raising. Loans are generally short term with the average loan size in the north ranging from dong 250,000 to dong 1 million. The smallest loan is dong 50,000, or about US$ 5. VBARD determines the eligibility of each borrower for being granted a loan. The lending rate is between 2.2 to 2.5 per cent per month with a spread of 0.7 per cent per month.

Deposits have been growing rapidly since the start of operations and by late 1994 represented 75 per cent of outstanding loans. Total deposits reached dong 530 billion (US$ 48 million) by the end of July 1996. People's Credit Funds have an appropriate incentive structure to make them self-sustained and attractive to large international agencies including ADB, which signed a US$ 20 million loan agreement with them in 1996.

(f) *Future prospects of the main formal financial institutions in rural areas*

Among the formal financial institutions in Viet Nam, VBARD, VBP and the People's Credit Funds are preferred formal financial institutions. They are governed by the Law on Banks and Financial Institutions and are directly supervised by the State Bank of Viet Nam. All of them, however, need to be restructured and strengthened in order to become self-funding.

VBARD changed its name in October 1996 to become a development bank and will move towards long-term financing and rural infrastructure investment. In order to achieve that objective, VBARD must be able to mobilize long-term deposits for long-term finance. The People's Credit Funds, based on their initial results, will increase from the current 1,000 to 2,000 by the year 2000, and become independent from State Bank of Viet Nam. VBP is now at a crossroads. Its first option is to end its current role as a financial institution and to become a welfare distributor, with continued subsidy from the government. The second option is to raise its interest rate and operate as a true financial institution. Implementing this second option will, however, cause it to overlap its operations with VBARD.

C. Impediments to the access of women to formal credit and financial institutions

According to the 1994 survey, "Statistics of situation on the development and income source of rural households in Viet Nam" carried out by GSO, female-headed households borrowed only 20 per cent of the total loans disbursed in rural areas (table III.12).

Table III.12. Distribution of loans by size of loan and by gender of household head (rural areas only)

Loan size (dong '000)	Sex of household head	
	Male (percentage)	Female (percentage)
1 000	78.24	21.76
2 000	80.43	19.57
3 000	81.54	18.46
4 000	89.38	10.62
5 000	79.55	20.45
10 000	91.30	8.70
20 000	88.71	19.92
Total	**80.08**	**19.92**

The survey indicates some critical differences in the credit status of men and women. The number of no-interest loans to female-headed households was just one-third of those to male-headed households. The average loan size obtained by women at rural financial institutions was less than half of the loans received by male counterparts.

With the exception of loans from government banks, the interest rates charged to women tended to be higher than the interest rates charged to men for all types of borrowing. The interest rates charged to enterprises run by women were also always higher than those charged to enterprises run by men. In the case of small businesses, the interest rate charges to women were triple the rates charged to men. Government banks, however, charge women less, not because women are a privileged group, but simply because the small number of women clients permits banks to offer small short-term loans at a lower interest rate. The majority of the men get larger long-term loans. For rural poor women, land is the most valuable property they possess. The survey, however, reported that the number of female landowners was only a third of the number of male landowners.

Due to the absence of gender-disaggregated data at Vietnamese banks and gender-focused polices by the government, assessing the access by women to formal credit and financial institutions is difficult. However, institutional or legal impediments and socio-cultural obstacles bar access by women.

1. Institutional and legal obstacles

Officially, government banks do not discriminate between men and women who borrow from government banks. Clients, however, often find bank procedures complex; consequently, loan applications filed by the less educated take longer to be approved. A case study done by UNDP revealed that it took a farmer in Nam Ha province four days to get a loan of dong 500,000 (US$ 45). When a woman borrows, she must prepare a plan indicating the purpose of her loan. The purpose of loans however are strictly regulated by banks. Of the loans requested by women, a large proportion is for consumption purposes which usually are not acceptable to banks (box III.3, case study 1). The economic activities of women are also regarded as low-income generating and small. (The 1994 census showed that while small and micro-enterprises headed by women accounted for 80 to 90 per cent of those enterprises, large businesses headed by men accounted for 90 per cent of such enterprises.) Finally, if the security for a loan is not adequate, banks will be reluctant to go through joint liability groups, a costly and complex type of credit delivery. A case study done in Tuyen Quang showed that formal financial institutions were unable to assist women's groups in enhancing their activities.

A major problem for women is the collateral requirement which is directly linked to the issue of property rights. In the 1992 Vietnamese Constitution, Article 6 states that "male and female citizens are equal in all aspects: political, economic, cultural and family", meaning that the wife has the same property and inheritance

---

Box III.3. Loan applications rejected by banks

Case study 1

In her application, a farming woman in Thanh Long commune, Tuyen Quang province, cited fish raising as the purpose for requesting a loan. The VBARD credit officer who visited her residence discovered, however, that there was no place to dig a fish pond. When questioned again regarding the purpose of the requested loan, the applicant said that she would actually buy a buffalo and plant lemon-grass. Having doubts over the applicant's explanation, the credit officer visited some of her neighbours and the commune People's Committee and discovered that Mrs Thu was pursuing a court case. Her husband had been killed in a land dispute and she had been a party in the suit. Her savings had been exhausted and she had turned to the bank. The applicant knew that the bank would never extend a loan for a non-productive purpose and she had therefore attempted to misrepresent the purpose of the loan. VBA rejected the loan application, citing falsification in the application.

Case study 2

A woman in Vinh Phu province applied for a loan, citing pig raising as the reason in her application. During a pre-loan check, the VBA credit officer found that the applicant, although a hard-working farmer, was poor, not well-educated and possessed no land, house or other property. The applicant had never had conflicts or legal problems with other people. To earn her living, she picked bamboo shoots and mushrooms, and logged timber for sale. Her income was thus unstable because of the seasonal nature of mushrooms and bamboo. VBA refused to approve the loan since it felt that giving loans to applicants with low and/or unstable incomes was risky.

rights as her husband. Furthermore, Articles 14 and 16 of the Ordinance on Marriage and Family note that if there is clear proof that property is owned by either the wife or her spouse, then it can be claimed by the rightful owner upon divorce. Otherwise, all possessions will be shared equally.

For the poor, the most valuable asset is land. The land title deed is, however, usually held under the name of a man. According to Vietnamese practice, this right is automatically transferred to the son(s), who have first priority of inheritance except when otherwise stated in the will. A daughter can inherit a piece of land from her parents but this seldom occurs since poor Vietnamese farmers do not own much land. Daughters have very few possessions when they marry and usually live at the home of the husband. Having no assets or power, women become dependent and inactive in economic activities. According to a census by GSO, female-headed households with land title deeds accounted for only 23 per cent of the total landowners. In rural households, women therefore accounted for only 4 per cent of the total loans with collateral. Since banks are also moving towards profit-based operations and loans are being extended on mortgage, female borrowers are placed at a further disadvantage (box III.3, case study 2).

Such difficulties make women clients hesitant to borrow from formal institutions. With regard to the obstacles mentioned above, four different types of financial contracts can be used: (a) loan contracts between banks and borrowers; (b) financial contracts between banks and donors; (c) financial contracts between banks and intermediaries; and (d) contracts between donors and intermediaries. Type (a) has already been addressed. Type (b) contracts are based on agreements between the Government of Viet Nam and the other parties concerned. Types (c) and (d) relate to group lending. For example, VBARD determines the criteria for selecting members, the mode of disbursement and collection, and the duties of each party for loans through women's groups. The returns for the intermediaries are stated in the contract either as a percentage of interest spread or as a fixed amount. Penalties are also imposed.

2. Sociocultural and geographical impediments

In Viet Nam, illiteracy or a lack of qualifications are the main sociocultural obstacles faced by women. Due to their limited education, many women find themselves unable to easily access formal credit. In rural areas, the education of a girl is considered "good for nothing" and that "the more a woman is educated, the more it is difficult for her to get married". Once she gets married, the kitchen or taking care of children are considered to be her domain, even though in reality women have to fulfill other income-generating duties. Credit markets in rural areas are not integrated because of a lack of information and their geographical separation, especially in the mountainous areas of the north, the central highlands and the island territories. In those parts of the country, the outreach of bank branches is still very limited. Poor and illiterate women are not aware of all the credit facilities available to them. Finally, formal credit agencies are often not interested in financing women clients, claiming that the return from women-invested projects is low and that they have to work hard to avoid delinquency.

D. Features of credit programmes with high female participation rates

Programmes with high female participation rates can be categorized as being either informal, formal or donor and NGO-led.

1. Informal programmes

As mentioned above, informal programmes comprise informal credit provided by friends and relatives, *tontines* and private moneylenders. The informal sector finances about 75 per cent of the total debts in Viet Nam. Women who face obstacles when obtaining credit from other sources are its main clients. A common feature of informal lending is high interest rates.

2. Programmes of the formal credit institutions

Lending policies of Vietnamese banks to individual borrowers are gender-neutral, thus posing some difficulties. Gender-disaggregated data could only be found in women's group lending by VWU and VBARD until 1995, when VBARD handed over joint liability group credit to VBP.

(a) *VBARD*

Since VBARD targets rural household lending, loans to individuals are rare. According to VBARD estimates, loans to female-headed households accounted for 30 per cent of its total loans. As of late 1995, those loans should have reached approximately 4 million female-headed households out of a total of 12 million households. According to the VBARD Annual Report for 1995, loans disbursed to farm households totalled dong 5,252,394,000,000 million as of December 1994 and dong 7,307,938 million as of December 1995. Funds granted to female-headed farm households are estimated at dong 1,575,718 million in 1994 and dong 2,192,381 million in 1995. Those loans were used mainly for crop production, poultry and livestock raising, food processing and small trading. Gender-disaggregated data regarding loan sizes, maturities and interest rates of those lending activities were unfortunately not covered by previous studies and were unavailable from the financial institutions. Those features therefore cannot be addressed in-depth by this study. Based on interviews with a number of VBARD bankers, most loans extended to women are short term, with a default rate of up to 0.5 per cent, which is much lower than the estimated 4 to 5 per cent for men.

(b) *Vietnam Women's Union*

Most of the reported credit and savings schemes with a high participation rate by women are linked to VBARD, VBP and VWU.

VWU was founded on 20 October 1930 as a quasi-governmental organization to operate at the central, provincial, district and communal levels. The first two levels form part of the government system. The number of VWU members totalled 11 million in 1994.[3] VWU serves as a social and financial intermediary between banks, donors, NGOs and joint liability groups; it provided loans to 1,960,000 members in 1995. VWU also implements various projects for women. Of the 54 projects funded by foreign NGOs in the period until 1995, VWU implemented 29 of the projects. The credit programmes initiated and directed by VWU during the period from 1989 to 1995 are reported in table III.13.

Table III.13. Vietnam Women's Union credit programmes, 1989-1995

Source of funds	Loan amount (million dong)	Communes reached	Women borrowers	Repeat women borrowers	Poor women borrowers
State budget	82 369	966	104 243	120 173	81 485
VBARD	687 392	3 108	509 289	572 056	371 533
External	42 419	931	102 913	143 344	81 361
VWU capital	50 330	4 081	360 616	460 720	218 945
Local credit and saving groups	156 959	4 812	617 390	995 514	420 952
Municipal budget	35 783	999	105 430	125 201	82 541
Other	49 990	737	136 354	194 406	119 471
Total	1 105 242	15 634	1 963 235	2 611 414	1 376 288

Source: Vietnam Women's Union data for two mobilizations, 1989-1995.

(c) *Features of women's group lending*

Funds for credit programmes by VWU come from different sources, with VBARD and joint liability groups equally accounting for about 30 per cent. Contributions from abroad are minor compared to domestic capital. Credit campaigns feature small loan amounts, interest rates which are competitive with market rates, a high recovery rate (95-100 per cent), high administration costs, loan purposes limited to production or service, and no requirement for collateral.

3. Donor agency and NGO programmes

There are also currently about 250 foreign NGOs in Viet Nam. At least 17 foreign and five local NGOs have reported implementing credit programmes to the rural poor. The total amount of grants reached US$ 4,160,000 in 1995 and involved about 75,900 women. Credit is accompanied by savings in those multi-purpose programmes. Loans can be used for reforestation, family planning or health care, or are determined by borrowers, as in the case of most NGO schemes.

---

[3] Document of the VII National Women's Congress.

NGOs schemes present some differences when compared to formal lending sources: (a) loan purposes are determined by borrowers; (b) foreign NGO funds are mainly donated and transferred to project holders at maturity if the recovery rate is high and objectives are obtained; (c) small in scope (an average loan value at dong 826,000 per person given to an average of 1,260 persons per project); (d) women from families without land or assets are provided with loans; (e) fund use and repayment schedules are closely monitored; (f) savings, training and technical assistance are integrated components of credit delivery; (g) there is a low rate of return on some financed projects; and (h) an operational cost that is higher than commercial lending.

4. Common features of all lending programmes

All of the above-mentioned programmes share a number of common features, including: (a) dominance by the informal sector; (b) programme design by the investors; (c) lending executed in conjunction with other programmes, such as family planning or health care; (d) short-term funds; (e) small loan value; (f) a higher collection rate compared to with male borrowers; (g) group lending with a high recovery rate; (h) a low return from invested projects; and (i) peer pressure substituting for traditional collateral.

5. Impact of credit schemes on poverty alleviation

The impact of savings and credit schemes on poverty alleviation is of crucial concern, but so far there has been no clear measurement of their impact. The schemes have not been implemented long enough to produce conclusive results, and it is difficult to measure the effects of other variables such as overall economic growth, new infrastructure or even the effects of other credit programmes. Many of the schemes provide insufficient data to make a structured comparison. Another issue pertains to the use of indicators for measuring poverty; some schemes are difficult to define and measure quantitatively.

Various institutions, however, have noted a number of positive impacts result-ing from the savings and credit schemes for women, including: (a) an improvement in the quality of life among the poor; (b) improved levels of household production (for example, a 36 per cent increase in livestock raised by UNICEF borrowers, compared to a 16 per cent increase for non-borrowers in 1996); (c) greater participation by women in household decision-making (UNFPA); (d) lower child malnutrition and higher primary school attendance (UNICEF); (e) increased knowledge of credit activities among women savers and credit group participants; (f) reduced female household debts (UNICEF); (g) improved access by poor women to the formal credit and financial sector; and (h) increased capacity in management by various government and non-government organizations such as VWU and the local People's Committees.

E. Relationship between formal credit and financial institutions and the public through intermediaries

Formal credit in Viet Nam can be channelled to the public via intermediaries, through the alternative models presented in figure III.2.

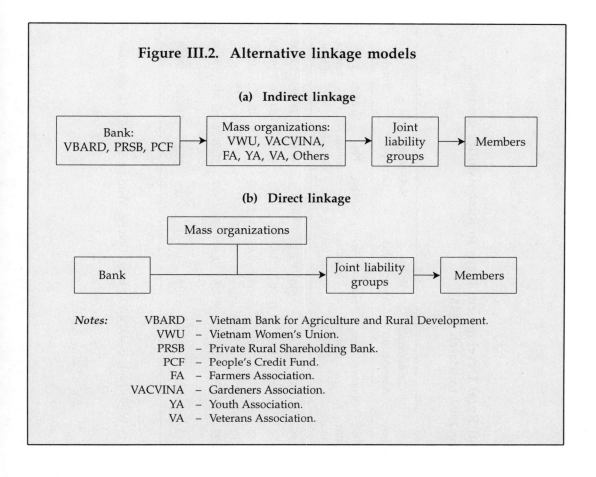

Figure III.2. Alternative linkage models

(a) Indirect linkage

Bank: VBARD, PRSB, PCF → Mass organizations: VWU, VACVINA, FA, YA, VA, Others → Joint liability groups → Members

(b) Direct linkage

Mass organizations

Bank → Joint liability groups → Members

Notes:		
VBARD	–	Vietnam Bank for Agriculture and Rural Development.
VWU	–	Vietnam Women's Union.
PRSB	–	Private Rural Shareholding Bank.
PCF	–	People's Credit Fund.
FA	–	Farmers Association.
VACVINA	–	Gardeners Association.
YA	–	Youth Association.
VA	–	Veterans Association.

1. Indirect linkage model

The indirect linkage model links VBARD, private rural shareholding banks, People's Credit Funds and, possibly, credit cooperatives with mass organizations. Mass organizations act as financial intermediaries between the banks and joint liability groups, and provide guidance and consultancy services, training services and financial intermediary services.

VWU is a suitable candidate for the role of financial intermediary given its extensive experience in savings and credit group organizing and management, promotion of group savings schemes, mediation with banks and financial extensions services, training of groups, and disbursement and collection of loans. However, VWU needs more training in areas of financial management, linkage banking, and the development of creative savings and credit schemes for each locality.

Mass organizations other than VWU, such as the Farmers Association or the Vietnam Association, may play the role of financial intermediary between banks and joint liability groups. These intermediaries may receive funding from VBARD (table III.14) and be involved as additional linkage partners. VWU can provide technical training courses to improve the capability of other mass organizations.

Table III.14. Vietnam Bank for Agriculture and Rural Development loans to joint liability groups by type (January 1994 to March 1995)

	Women's Group		Farmers Association		Veterans Association		Gardeners Association		Youth Association		Self-Help Group		Total	
	Number	Per-centage of total	Number	Per-centage of total	Number	Per-centage of total	Number	Per-centage of total	Number	Per-centage of total	Number	Per-centage of total	Number	Per-centage of total
Number of groups	10 949	28.78	12 776	33.58	336	0.88	17	0.04	846	2.22	13 124	34.49	38 048	100.00
Number of members	266 961	38.77	182 241	26.47	6 199	0.90	721	0.10	11 245	1.63	221 171	32.12	688 538	100.00
Number of passbooks	49 735	46.33	31 085	28.96	915	0.85	7	0.01	10	0.01	25 600	23.85	107 352	100.00
Loans granted (in D million)	243 278	22.88	397 789	37.41	9 795	0.92	350	0.03	10 355	0.97	401 674	37.78	1 063 241	100.00
Loans outstanding (in D million)	135 877	24.87	188 829	34.57	6 112	1.12	325	0.06	6 042	1.11	209 086	38.28	546 261	100.00

Source: Vietnam Bank for Agriculture and Rural Development.
Sources of loans for VBARD lending to groups: VBARD funds, World Bank, IFAD, RABO bank, UNFPA, Vietcombank, SBV, Government of Germany.

2. Direct linkage model

In the direct linkage model, banks are linked directly with the joint liability groups which function as financial intermediaries between members (farmers and micro-enterpreneurs) and banks. In this linkage scheme, the groups provide guidance and consultancy services to their member-borrowers as well as training and financial intermediation. The mass organizations provide consultancy services and directives, check eligibility of borrowers in cooperation with the local People's Committees, and monitor credit flow. VBARD provides 90 per cent of the formal sector funding in rural areas and also provides funding for group lending through mass organizations (table III.14).

F. Relationship between the formal credit and financial institutions, and donor agencies and non-governmental organizations

1. Role of donor agencies

The role of donor agencies in microfinancing in Viet Nam is rather complex, as shown in figure III.3.

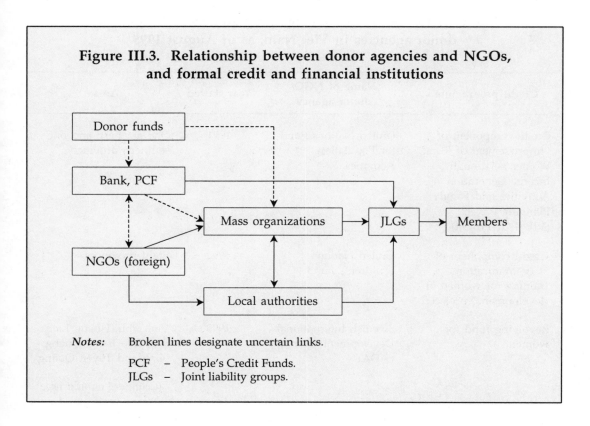

Figure III.3. Relationship between donor agencies and NGOs, and formal credit and financial institutions

Notes: Broken lines designate uncertain links.

PCF – People's Credit Funds.
JLGs – Joint liability groups.

The linkage between donor agencies and formal financial institutions determines the modalities of current programmes. Donor funds may come from bilateral programmes, multilateral programmes and NGOs.

A well-known bilateral programme is the Family Planning Project funded by the Australian Family Planning Association (FPA) for VWU, which terminated on 29 February 1996. The two parties had signed an agreement for a loan to VWU of $A 1,395,273. VWU then entered into a financial contract with VBARD, where the amount of US$ 50,000 from the loan proceeds were to be deposited with VBARD as a guarantee fund. The guarantee fund covered 75 per cent of possible losses incurred, while the remaining 25 per cent was shouldered by VBARD, which acted as the direct lender for group lending. The local People's Committee and the local VWU checked the eligibility of group members. VBARD paid the joint-liability groups 6 per cent commission on the total interest.

Another example is the Viet Nam-Sweden forestry programme which operated from 1991 to 1995. Total donor funds of US$ 163,620 were channelled to farm households directly from the project, through intermediaries, and through VBARD. VBARD thus acted as a direct lender, using the available funds.

Under those projects, a formal financial institution (VBA) was a co-lender with the donor(s). Donor credit programmes are listed in table III.15.

Table III.15. Credit and savings programmes of NGOs and donor agencies in Viet Nam, as of August 1995

Credit programme	Name of NGO/ donor agency	Year started	Area
Credit component of "Improvement of Rural Women's Through Income Generation Activities and Family Planning Project" (VIE/PO1 Project)	United Nations Fund for Population Activities	1991	One northern and one southern province
Credit component of "Communication training for women in development" project	United Nations Children's Fund	1992	Eight provinces
Revolving fund for women	Swedish International Development Agency (SIDA)	1990	Vinh Phu, Hoang Lien Son, Cao Bang, Quang Ninh and Tuyen Quang

(Continued on next page)

56

Table III.15 (continued)

Credit programme	Name of NGO/ donor agency	Year started	Area
Commune based credit and savings programme	Save the Children Fund/UK (SCF/UK)	1990	Thang Chuong, Cam Xuyen
Savings and credit projects in five communes	World Vision	1991	Two districts of Hue province
Programme for the Reintegration of Vietnamese Returnees from Asylum Countries	European Community (EC)	1992	First phase: Hai Phong, Quang Ninh, Ho Chi Minh City
Savings and credit projects in five communes	Menmonite Central Committee (MCC)	1992	Two districts in Vinh Phu province
Quang Ninh Income Generation Project for Women	CARE International	1993	Four districts in Quang Ninh province
Savings and credit projects in four provinces	Oxfam – Belgique	1993	Five districts in three provinces: Ha Tinh, Nghe An, Ha Bac
Savings and credit project in Nghe An and Vinh Phu	Catholic Relief Services (CRS)	1993	Two districts in Nghe An and Vinh Phu provinces
Affection Fund (TYM)	Cooperation Internationale Pour le Developpement Et La Solidarite (CIDSE), World Relief, Oxfam, CRS, Japanese NGOs	1992	Southern provinces of Viet Nam
Credit Scheme for Poor Farmer Households	French Vietnamese Association	1993	Six villages in four districts in northern Viet Nam
Rural Supervised Credit Pilot Project	Rabobank and FMO	1993	Three provinces: Ha Nam Ninh, Nghe Tinh and An Giang
Pilot Project in Son La Province	Action Aid Vietnam	1993	Mai Son district, Son La province

2. Role of NGOs

The linkage model becomes complex with the participation of NGOs. Some NGOs choose banks or People's Credit Funds as partners while others give direct loans to borrowers. According to the 1995 NGOs Forum Data however, only 5 per cent of the projects which aimed to graduate borrowers to the formal financial sector had links with banks. For projects linked with VBARD, namely JIVC 95-0027 and a number of CIDSE schemes, VBARD was the implementor and direct lender. The funds could be revolved for new borrowers or transferred to project beneficiaries like the local People's Committees.

3. Strengthening links between government organizations and NGOs

The success of microfinance schemes always depends on the strength of the links between local government agencies, and between those agencies and NGOs and mass organizations. Most the foreign NGO schemes reported facing difficulties with local authorities over the targeting of the poor. This problem arose from the fact that local authorities in many of the schemes were supposed to ensure that the initial capital, which may have been provided as a grant, would continue to be used for lending to the poor after the end of each project. According to the Savings and Credit Forum of Viet Nam, the initial capital in many NGO projects was to be given to the project holders upon project completion as an incentive for local authorities to take part in the programmes.

A related issue concerns the choice of local partner for project management and implementation. The credibility of a savings and credit scheme is likely to be closely linked to the credibility of local partners. The most common local partner is VWU, although others such as the People's Committees, the Farmers Association and local branches of VBARD have been chosen. Mass organizations have been reported as being more effective local partners than the People's Committees. However, even with a mass organization such as VWU, considerable differences in performance are reported in different regions. One issue affecting VWU is the sheer number of partnerships that the organization has entered into with various donors and government agencies. In some areas, the limited numbers of VWU staff are overloaded by simultaneous donor schemes. The schemes may have different rules and reporting requirements, or may be aimed at similar target groups, thus impeding the capability of VWU if staff members are not well trained.

To tighten the links between NGOs and government organizations in the field, the following measures are recommended:

(a) NGOs, together with domestic mass organizations and foreign organizations, should coordinate closely in the areas of financing. At the moment, a large proportion of funds goes to VWU. VWU should redistribute some of its credit and savings schemes to other mass organizations, such as FA and VACVINA. Since other mass organizations are not yet capable of undertaking such schemes, VWU or other agencies should train them in financial management;

(b) Government organizations, comprising the local People's Committee, local sectoral agencies like the Department of Agriculture, and academic institutions like the Agriculture Extension Station and the Viet Nam Institute for Agricultural Science and Technology should be more active in consultancy and training services for joint liability groups, in collaboration with mass organizations and banks. As reported above, many groups lack accounting skills;

(c) The People's Committees should act as the overall leader in loan monitoring, and most importantly, loan collection. People's Committees should regularly attend and assist group meetings. People's Committees should also report the impact of the programmes to the next higher level, to align them with the local master development plan. The People's Committees and the government should create a sustainable legal framework within which NGOs can operate and, without violating Vietnamese laws, should remove obstacles faced by NGOs. Related to this issue, Decision No. 340/TTG of May 1996, which concerns regulations for foreign NGO operations in Viet Nam, is highly appreciated and should help to tighten links between NGOs and various agencies in Viet Nam;

(d) NGOs should improve their links with the formal financial sector. Of the 60 NGO-funded projects in Viet Nam in 1995, only three projects by CIDSE and World Vision reported ties with formal banks. Improving links with banks will help NGO borrowers in their transition in using formal sector facilities;

(e) NGOs should work out a procedure for measuring the impact of their schemes on the beneficiaries.

G. Recommendations for providing sustainable microcredit to women

Since many parties are involved in the provision of credit to poor women, the sustainability of each is crucial to ensure the sustainability of the programmes as a whole. A sustainable microfinance linkage should be viewed through the sustainability of intermediaries, formal credit and financial institutions.

1. Sustainability of intermediaries

Intermediaries, and particularly VWU, face problems of poor management, a lack of clear ownership and irregular funding. Banking services offered by the District Women's Union is poor and many of the management functions are relegated to foreign NGOs. The capacity of VWU in management and banking should be strengthened to enable the organization to fulfil its tasks and obtain the confidence of banks and foreign donors, even after the withdrawal of its foreign partners.

A lack of clear ownership means that it is unclear as to who should enjoy the profits from the schemes and who should take the responsibility for losses. It is recommended that a distinct financial contract or directive, which clearly delineates the functional responsibilities among the units involved, be formulated within a legal framework designed by the relevant agencies.

NGOs face the problem of self-sustainability since their funds are irregular concessional funds. Once the NGOs withdraw, the project results which had been obtained by hard effort can simply fade away. It is recommended that in order to achieve and maintain stable operations, NGOs should form close links with banks to ensure the continuity of fund sourcing.

2. Sustainability of formal credit institutions

It is important that current economic policies and practices assist formal credit institutions to become sustainable. It was stated above that VBARD and VBP, and even the People's Credit Funds, face a dilemma over covering costs or meeting social welfare objectives, and a range of reforms need to be designed and implemented. Ensuring the sustainability of those institutions requires the implementation of accurate and prudential revisions in macroeconomic policies and enabling environment, as well as institutions and organizations, networks and processes, financial management and human resources.

(a) *Macroeconomic policies and enabling environment*

Macroeconomic policies affecting microfinance, particularly those which affect credit and savings among poor women who have limited access to formal credit, need to be revisited. It is questionable whether subsidized credit is the best mechanism for income transfers to rural areas and the poor. The definition of "market" interest rates when most lending is set at fixed rates is unclear. What are the alternative policies that the government can adopt to assist the poor who have little capacity for productive investments and repayment? The distortions and additional costs of below-market lending at different fixed rates should be defined, the real costs of borrowing calculated, and comparisons made of possible alternatives. For example, a direct subsidy to the poor as a type of income transfer may help minimize distortions in the financial markets. The provision of better information, physical infrastructure, well-designed laws and property rights, and credit at market interest rates will minimize risks and improve access of poor women to formal credit and financial institutions.

Problems are encountered in setting interest rates. The present 0.35 per cent spread between the interest rates on deposit and loans, as set by VBARD and VBP, is far too small for sustainable microfinance activity. Based on the experience of People's Credit Funds, which offer the most sustainable institution, the margin should be 0.7 per cent. According to VBARD, given the fierce competition in financial markets, this spread could be reduced to 0.5 per cent, which is still reasonable and profitable. Other bureaucratic controls like individual bank credit ceilings and different taxation regimes (VBP) prevent formal financial sector institutions from responding to market price signals, and they act like rent-seeking enterprises under the centrally-planned economy.

The hunger elimination and poverty reduction programmes of the government aim to provide 90 to 95 per cent of the loans to poor households, at about dong 1 million for each household, by the year 2000. However, it is unclear as to how the households classified as "extremely poor" will be able to invest in productivity and repay loans under these programmes. This form of financing does not seem to be sustainable and if the credit is granted on a one-time basis, it will not be available to all, and especially the poor in isolated regions.

The government should take the initiative in comprehensively reviewing VBARD activities to date. The review should determine the interest rate which can cover loan costs (including the interest on deposits), operational costs and the provision for bad debts and losses. Even if agreement is reached on an interest rate spread of 0.5 per cent, differential rates may need to be charged, based on risk assessments. Finally, donor programmes for VBARD should be coordinated with a strategic development and training plan in mind. A structure for assistance, incorporating bi-monthly meeting of VBARD donors, could also be initiated.

(b) *Institutions and organizations*

There is little point in classifying VBP as a formal financial institution. Judging from current VBP practices, the institution behaves more like a welfare distributor than a bank. All aspects of the bank, such as its organization, interests for loans and deposits, and target clients are controlled by the government. According to the opinions of the various agencies, the development of VBP has been installed. An urgent concern is whether VBP should establish its own network of agencies in parallel to the VBARD network which currently acts as the VBP agency network. A complex duplication of facilities seems unnecessary.

People's Credit Funds are rapidly expanding in Viet Nam. The central People's Credit Fund still relies heavily on the State Bank of Viet Nam; the People's Credit Fund chairman is deputy governor of the State Bank of Viet Nam. The People's Credit Funds extend loans for various purposes without collateral, and consumption loans account for 4 per cent of the total outstanding loans. Since People's Credit Funds are a relatively new innovation, their staff do not have enough experience and compared to bank staff are not as qualified. Training for staff would improve their capacity to compete with other financial institutions. The supervision capacity of People's Credit Funds by the State Bank of Viet Nam is currently stretched and is inadequate to meet the substantial increase in their activities. A new organizational structure is required at the State Bank of Viet Nam in order to improve supervision and prevent the mismanagement which led to the end of credit cooperatives in the late 1980s. Some senior People's Credit Fund officials believe that long-term sustainability can be ensured by establishing a security fund from a percentage of total deposits. The Funds are also piloting a deposit insurance programme to promote trust by its members.

Formal microfinance institutions in Viet Nam should explore the possibilities of concessionary funding from international agencies such as ADB, the World Bank and UNDP, which have been active in providing technical assistance to VBARD. At this stage, the absorptive capacity of key government institutions should be considered by the government at the central level.

An exchange of experiences with neighbouring countries should be utilized to facilitate solving these issues. Workshops and seminars on microfinance and the role of women should be organized. The participation of VBARD and VBP staff involved in business planning, as well as central bank staff and other policy makers, is crucial.

(c) *Networks and processes*

The level of formal sector savings in Viet Nam is low compared with other countries which have high bank savings rates even in rural areas. The low trust placed in Vietnamese banks and the limited access to facilities need to be understood and remedied. At VBP, women clients are often faced with a complex, non-streamlined approval process which prevents easy access, since "poverty committees" are involved at different levels.

The actual role and activities of the informal sector also need to be realized. As noted in the above sections, once the role of the informal sector is well-defined and understood, competition between the formal, semi-formal and informal sectors should increase and thus reduce the scope for "unfair" lending practices. Also, with regard to outreach, poor women may never get to a VBARD branch, even if they are aware of it, as a result of difficult terrain in the areas where they live.

(d) *Financial management*

A new accounting system which was to be adopted by VBARD has been delayed. The financial forecasting and reporting systems, and the management reporting systems of VBP and People's Credit Funds are still poor or inadequate. Those management and monitoring systems will have to be strengthened if they are to meet international standards. Formal financial institutions should remember and learn from the mismanagement which led to the failure of credit cooperatives in the late 1980s. Over-expansion and overly optimistic assumptions must be avoided. All formal credit institutions should ensure that their financial management is based on conservative estimates of repayment rates.

(e) *Human resources*

Microfinance schemes in Viet Nam are constrained by the lack of qualified credit and finance officers in VBARD, VBP and the People's Credit Funds. This lack signals the need for on-the-job training, refresher courses and the extension of training to credit group members. Similar training should also be considered for non-government organizations.

Mass organizations currently have limited management skills so they cannot help their members to operate large-scale enterprises Based on the 1994 General Statistics Office Census, only 8 per cent of large businesses in the countryside are run by women. Women should be trained so that they can work competitively with men. Bank branches should be able to train them in maintaining savings and credit accounts, as well as provide production knowledge, especially at the grassroots level.

3. Recommendations for improving access by poor women to formal credit

Since various impediments remain to the access by poor women to the formal financial sector, the following recommendations are suggested:

(a) An enabling environment should be created for women to participate in credit and savings activities. At the macro level the government should design women-focused policies and appoint banks as implementors. The government should seek more foreign donors funds for such programmes;

(b) Banks should change their attitude towards women borrowers. In order to accomplish this objective satisfactorily, gender-disaggregated data, especially for commercial lending, should be maintained by banks and financial institutions. Banks should initiate pilot projects for removing hurdles and measuring possible impacts on women. A certain percentage of bank loan portfolios should also be set aside as finance for women. VWU and banks should also make women aware of the different conditions and interest rates offered by existing financial facilities (table III.16).

(c) The development of rural finance should promote competition among lenders. The formal sector should take into account the comparative advantage of each institution. All formal sector lending should be at market interest rates (table III.16) and should aim at minimizing transaction costs. Case studies and interviews with VBP and VBARD indicate that poor women can cope with market interest rates. Furthermore, poor women currently find it difficult to borrow at lower-than-market interest rates. Being able to access loans as easily as men will better assist women.

Table III.16. Viet Nam: Average interest rates by lenders and by enterprise size

(Unit: percentage per month)

Type of lender	Enterprise		Total
	Micro	Small	
Moneylenders	8.6	6.4	8.4
Relatives	0.8	1.0	0.8
Private individuals	1.8	1.3	1.7
Private banks	1.1	...	1.1
Government banks	2.6	2.8	2.6
Cooperatives	2.9	0.0	2.6
Others	1.1	...	1.1
Total	**3.3**	**2.5**	**3.3**

Source: General Statistics Office, 1994.

(d) To reach to poor women, banks should expand their networks, especially in remote areas. Banks should also effect changes in attitude and in the structure of their premises. Banking procedures should be simplified. Bank staff should complete the forms for women, if necessary, and should explain the procedures to them. The current style of transaction offices creates a barrier between the clients and banks, and should be replaced by interview tables that create a friendlier atmosphere for women borrowers.

(e) Institutional and legal impediments should be removed. The current most effective model of microfinance for women is group lending. Group formation, therefore, needs to be strengthened. Joint liability group members, especially leaders and bookkeepers, should be well-trained. Economic expertise must be provided to group members to enable them to become good managers in production and banking procedures. This goal can be achieved by closer coordination between banks and mass organizations. Peer pressure in group loans should be considered as a substitute for traditional collateral. If that principle can be applied, VBARD will be able to finance the large body of potential women clients.

(f) Assistance from NGOs should be applied to group formation and various lending practices. Based on government Decision No. 340/TTG, dated 24 May 1996, VWU and related agencies will be able to strengthen links with NGOs and access their funds.

Changes to improve access by women to the formal financial sector should be implemented in two stages. In the first stage, an indirect linkage, as discussed above, can be implemented and a transition made to the direct linkage model. During the trial period, banks should grant small loans for measuring the impact on poverty and classifying clientele, as well as for determining training needs and the impediments to be removed in subsequent programmes. Once women become familiar with financial and production procedures, they can move to larger businesses and become independent borrowers. Credit and investment should be tied to savings since the latter is necessary to create equity for future projects. Since credit is not a grant, loan use should strictly monitored. More pilot programmes should be carried out to obtain feedback and experience.

In the second stage, women will have already obtained their own assets and skills for conducting a business. However, in dealing with technical and financial matters they will still need assistance from banks, academic institutions and local authorities. Current institutional and legal obstacles, such as limited property rights, need to be gradually revised. During this period, banks should consider extending larger loans to female-headed enterprises. To ensure the repayment of such loans, a Guarantee Fund is needed. The capital for the fund could be obtained from joint liability group members of the municipal budget.

BIBLIOGRAPHY

Abiad, V.G. *Grassroots Financial Systems Development in Vietnam.* October 1995.

Johnson, Alan. *Microfinance in Viet Nam.* May 1996.

Nichols, Paul. *Social Survey Methods.* Oxfam, 1991.

Seibel, Hans Dieter. *Strategies for Developing Viable Microfinance Institutions and Sustainable Microfinancial Services in Asia.* (APRACA/GTZ), mimeographed.

Viet Nam. *Civil Law of Viet Nam.* (Hanoi, State Politics Publishing House) 1995.

Viet Nam. *Savings and Credit Forum of Viet Nam.* (Hanoi, unpublished) 1995.

Villareal, F.L. *Women in Rural Savings and Finance.* United Nations Development Programme (RAS/88/PO7), mimeographed.

World Bank. *Viet Nam Financial Sector Review.* 1 March 1995. (Report No. 13135-VN).

World Bank. *Vietnam Fiscal Decentralization and the Delivery of Rural Services.* 31 October 1996. (Report No. 15745-VN).

World Bank. *Vietnam Poverty Assessment and Strategy.* 1995.

QUESTIONNAIRE AND ANSWERS FROM FIELD VISITS UNDERTAKEN IN TUYEN QUANG, HA TAY AND VINH PHU PROVINCES

1. **What are the requirements for a woman to borrow from VBARD/VBP?**

   VBARD requirements:

   (a) Women must have submitted a loan application.

   (b) Women must have a production/business project and be a resident in the locality.

   (c) Women must have some initial capital of their own.

   (d) Women borrowing less than dong 1 million do not need to have collateral.

   (e) Women borrowing over dong 1 million must have collateral.

   VBP requirements:

   (a) Only families named in the poverty alleviation list issued by the poverty alleviation committee in villages, wards, towns, and chosen by the chairman of the local People's Committee, can be guaranteed a loan. In addition, they must also be approved by the representative of the VBP management board.

   (b) Poor households do not need collateral but they have to be guaranteed by the "lending and saving groups" or social and political organizations (which means that they have to join the groups).

   (c) Poor borrowers must live in the countryside or in a town having a branch office of VBP.

   (d) Women must prepare a loan application.

   (e) A woman can only receive a new loan when she has repaid the old debt.

2. **When a woman wants to take out a loan, does she need to have her husband's signature before the loan application is approved?**

   (a) VBARD does not require her husband's signature before the loan application is approved.

   (b) VBP asks for the legitimate person's signature before the loan application is approved.

3. **Can a woman inherit a piece of land from her parents?**

   Yes, she can.

4. **Can the land title deed be in her name only?**

   No, it cannot. The land title deed must include her name and those of the family members.

5. **Can she use the land title deed to borrow from the bank?**

   Yes, she can.

6. **Are there any restrictions on borrowing by a woman?**

   She must utilize the loan for investing in a small-scale project.

7. **Does VBARD/VBP keep a record of borrowers by gender; for example, how many borrowers in 1996 were women?**

   No, it does not, but VWU keeps a record of borrowers in its annual report.

8. **What are the most common types of loans made by women?**

   Loans must be used for the such purposes as livestock purchases/raising, small-scale business, cultivation etc.

9. **In Tuyen Quang, what are the major impediments or obstacles to the ability of women to borrow from the banks?**

   (a) The banks require borrowers have to be enough supporting material, but since the knowledge of women is lower, they find it difficult to prepare the documentation.

   (b) Formal credit organizations and microfinancing institutions are not strong enough to help women's group to enhance their activities.

   (c) Productivity in livestock cultivation by women is not high and living standards are lower, so they have to work hard to repay the bank.

10. **Based on your experience in banking, which group of borrowers are better at making payments, men or women?**

    Women's groups can make better payments because they keep money in their families, and they can save and economize. In addition, they can do many other things better than men.

11. **In your opinion, how can access by women to formal (bank) credit be further improved?**

    (a) Expand the banking network.

    (b) Ensure closer coordination between mass organizations and formal banks.

    (c) Form self-help groups of borrowers.

    (d) Make the procedures more simple.

12. **What are the characteristics of credit programmes with a high participation of women?**

They are:

(a) The designated programmes by the investors.

(b) Mixed programmes: a lending programme is executed together with another programme (family planning, health care etc.).

(c) Programmes with various activities, such as lending and saving, for which joint liability among the members is very high.

13. **What are the categories of women who find it difficult to obtain loans at banks in Hatay and Hai Phong provinces?**

(a) Women in families where the members (parents or husbands) have violated laws such as tax laws, or who have overdue debts at other financial institutions.

(b) Women in families having disputes over land or other property.

(c) Women under the threat of separation or divorce.

(d) Women or their husbands with problems related to substance abuse or gambling.

ANNEX II   LIST OF AGENCIES VISITED AND PERSONS INTERVIEWED

1. **State Bank of Viet Nam:**

   - Ms Tuong, Manager of Statistical Bureau, Department of Economics Research.

2. **Vietnam Bank for the Poor:**

   - Mrs Nguyen Thi Thin, Deputy Director-General;
   - Mrs Huong, Deputy Manager of the Credit Department.

3. **Vietnam Bank for Agriculture and Rural Development:**

   - Mr Cam Hieu Kien, Deputy General-Director;
   - Mr Trung, Mr Hung, Mr Ngu, Credit Department.

4. **Vietnam Women's Union:**

   - Mrs Nguyen Thi Tan, Propaganda and Family Planning Committee.

5. **People's Aids Coordination Committee:**

   - Mr Phong.

READERSHIP SURVEY

The Development Research and Policy Analysis Division of ESCAP is undertaking an evaluation of the publication: *Improving the Access of Women to Formal Credit and Financial Institutions: Windows of Opportunity, Volume II*, with a view to improving the usefulness of future publications to our readers. We would appreciate it if you could complete this questionnaire and return it, at your earliest convenience, to

Director
Development Research and Policy Analysis Division
ESCAP, United Nations Building
Rajadamnern Avenue
Bangkok 10200, THAILAND

QUESTIONNAIRE

Rating for quality and usefulness (please circle)	Excellent	Very good	Average	Poor
1. Please indicate your assessment of the *quality* of the publication on:				
• presentation/format	4	3	2	1
• readability	4	3	2	1
• timeliness of information	4	3	2	1
• coverage of subject matter	4	3	2	1
• analytical rigour	4	3	2	1
• overall guality	4	3	2	1
2. How *useful* is the publication to your work?				
• provision of information	4	3	2	1
• clarification of issues	4	3	2	1
• its findings	4	3	2	1
• policy suggestions	4	3	2	1
• overall usefulness	4	3	2	1

3. Please give examples of how this publication has contributed to your work:

....

....

....

4. Suggestions for improvement of the publication:

    ....

    ....

    ....

5. Your background information, please,

    Name: ....

    Title/position: ....

    Institution: ....

    Office address: ....

Please use additional sheets of paper if required to answer the questions. Thank you for your kind cooperation in completing this questionnaire.

This publication may be obtained from:

Director
Development Research and Policy Analysis Division
Economic and Social Commission for Asia and the Pacific
The United Nations Building
Rajadamnern Avenue, Bangkok 10200, Thailand

Tel: (662) 288-1610
Fax: (662) 288-3007
Telex: 82392 ESCAP TH, 82315 ESCAP TH
E-mail: islam.unescap@un.org
Cable: ESCAP BANGKOK